Kimberly Elam

Princeton Architectural Press, New York

DESIGN BRIEFS IIII|IIIIIIIIIIIII *ESSENTIAL TEXTS ON DESIGN*

ALSO AVAILABLE IN THIS SERIES:

D.I.Y. Design It Yourself, by Ellen Lupton

Elements of Design, by Gail Greet Hannah

Geometry of Design, by Kimberly Elam

Thinking with Type, by Ellen Lupton

Typographic Systems, by Kimberly Elam

Visual Grammar, by Christian Leborg

Published by
Princeton Architectural Press
37 East Seventh Street
New York, New York 10003

For a free catalog of books, call 1.800.722.6657.
Visit our web site at www.papress.com.

Project Editors: Linda Lee and Jennifer N. Thompson
Design: Kimberly Elam
Cover Design: Deb Wood

Special thanks to: Nettie Aljian, Nicola Bednarek, Janet Behning,
Megan Carey, Penny (Yuen Pik) Chu, Russell Fernandez, Jan
Haux, Clare Jacobson, John King, Mark Lamster, Nancy Eklund
Later, Katharine Myers, Jane Sheinman, Scott Tennent, Joseph
Weston, and Deb Wood of Princeton Architectural Press
—Kevin C. Lippert, publisher

.

Library of Congress Cataloging-in-Publication Data

Elam, Kimberly, 1951–
 Grid systems : principles of organizing type / Kimberly Elam.
    p. cm.
 Includes index.
 ISBN 978-1-56898-465-0 (pbk. : alk. paper)
 1. Graphic design (Typography) 2. Type and type-founding.
 I. Title.

 Z246.E534 2003
 686.2'2—dc22

                                                      2004001242

Table of Contents

5	Introduction
7	Project Elements and Process
8	Constraints and Options
9	Proportion of Elements
10	Grouping
11	Negative Space and Grouping
12	Perimeter Edge and Axial Relationships
13	The Law of Thirds
14	The Circle and Composition
17	Horizontal Composition
35	Brochure for *Die Neue Typographie*
36	Cover Page and Text Page from *The Isms of Art*
37	Spread from the Catalog of Bauhaus Products
38	Theatre Am Hechtplatz Advertisement
40	SamataMason Web Site
42	Institute for Architecture and Urban Studies Graphic Program
44	Sotheby's Graphic Program
45	Table of Contents Spread for *The New Urban Landscape*
46	Horizontal/Vertical Composition
63	*Zürcher Künstler im Helmhaus* Poster
64	Nike ACG Pro Purchase Catalog
66	Program for Zurich University's 150th Anniversary
67	*Best Swiss Posters of the Year 1992*
68	*Festival d'été* (Summer Festival), Program Spread
69	Columbia University, Graduate School of Architecture and Planning Posters
71	Diagonal Composition
89	Kandinsky Poster
90	Page from *Reklama Mechano*
90	Page from *The Next Call*
91	*National-Zeitung* (Newspaper) Poster Series
92	Title Page Studies for the Freiburg Municipal Theatre
94	Columbia University, Graduate School of Architecture and Planning, Lecture and Exhibition Posters
97	Typographic Hierarchy
104	Case Study: Identification of the AIDS Virus
107	Case Study: The Beginning of Communism in Cuba
112	Case Study: Levi's Become Fashion
116	Case Study: "If the glove don't fit, you must acquit."
118	Acknowledgments
118	Image Credits
118	Selected Bibliography
119	Index

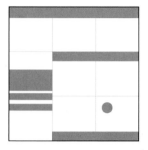

Typography is not only verbal information but also lines of texture within a composition. These textures create rectangles of tone on the page, and the relationship of the positions of these rectangles is critical to the perception of order and unity within a composition. The duality of the two roles gives the designer responsibility for both communication and composition.

This typography project enables the designer to focus and explore the role of composition within a system and a structure. The structure is a simple three-column by three-row grid system. Although this is a modest system, there is enough flexibility for variation and thorough investigation. The 3 X 3 grid system also corresponds to the law of thirds that suggests when a rectangle or square is divided into thirds vertically and horizontally, the four intersecting points within the composition are the points of optimal focus. The designer uses placement and proximity to determine which of these points is hierarchically the most important.

The example at left is a simple composition of six rectangles and a small circle. The elements are in proportion to each other and are grouped and arranged in the grid so that each rectangular element aligns with at least one other element. The interior alignments, proportion of elements, and placement in the format result in a unified and visually satisfying composition. In this example, the gray rectangles have been replaced by lines of text. There is an obvious hierarchy in the content of the message, via text size and placement, and an alignment axis at the left of the format. Analysis of these three samples shows that the compositional principles related to typographic messages are the same in all. An understanding of the compositions abstract elements of texture leads the designer to a deeper understanding of the role of the compositional principles and visual forces of design. This project is a case study of a methodology used to teach these principles and visual forces.

This book, and others in the series, is indebted to my students for all they have taught me and is intended to share with others approaches and methodology that may prove useful. Design education is a fluid process that constantly evolves. Designers and design educators are invited to share the results of their experiences with me for inclusion in later printings of this work.

Kimberly Elam

Ringling School of Art and Design
Department of Graphic and Interactive Communication
Sarasota, Florida

A three-column by three-row structure is the format for exploring texture and composition. This simple grid system provides a wide range of variation for exploration within a controlled system of organization. Because the format is a square, visual attention will focus on the interior composition rather than the shape and proportion of the format.

Six gray rectangles, which will later correspond to the type sizes of the visual message, are the compositional elements. A small circle is also used to provide an element for balance, visual control of the composition, and contrast.

The circle is the wild-card element in all of the compositions. Even though it is very small, it has a tremendous amount of visual power. This is true of any circle, any size, in just about any composition. The human eye loves the circle and embraces it. The contrast in form to the rectangular elements provides visual interest, in addition to the inherent visual power of the circle itself. Its position in the composition is less prescribed than the other elements, and it can appear anywhere.

The student explores the visual principles of composition, texture, and interrelationship through a series of exercises that become increasingly complex and dynamic.

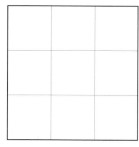

The grid system is three columns wide by three rows deep, yielding a total of nine visual fields.

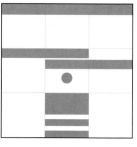

The compositional elements are six gray rectangles and a small circle.

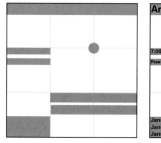

The compositional elements are arranged within the grid system.

Lines of text replace the gray compositional elements (above) and yield a typographic composition (below).

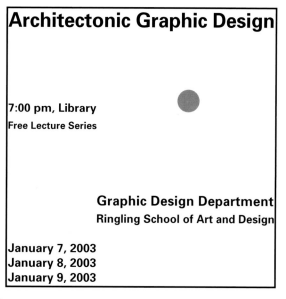

The format, rectangle elements, and a concise series of rules are given to the student:
- In the horizontal series, all rectangle elements must remain on the horizontal. In the horizontal/vertical series, all rectangles must be either horizontal or vertical. In the diagonal series, all rectangles must be on the same or contrasting diagonal.
- All rectangle elements must be used.
- No rectangle element may extend outside the format.
- Rectangle elements may almost touch but not overlap.

Since this is a formal composition project, the constraints are important rules for creating a cohesive whole. Elements must remain on the horizontal in the first series and will occupy other positions in later series. It is important that all elements are used, as each bar corresponds to a line of text from a message that will later replace the rectangle elements. All elements are sized to fit in either one, two, or three visual fields and must fit, left to right, within the grid columns.

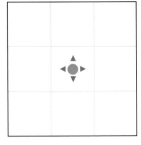
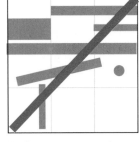
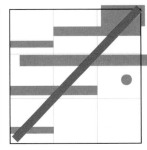
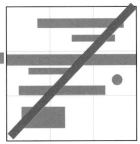

Yes. All rectangle elements are on the horizontal and all elements are used. Elements do not extend beyond the format or overlap. The circle may be placed anywhere in the format but may not overlap other elements.

No. Elements must remain on the horizontal for the first series. Later compositions will work with vertical and diagonal elements.

No. Elements may never overlap or extend beyond the format perimeter.

No. Elements must fit within the grid columns.

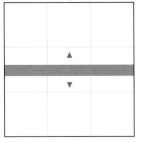
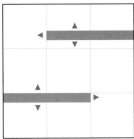
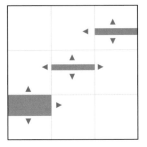

The circle may occupy any position. It is a wild-card element in the composition and need not necessarily correspond to the grid lines.

The largest rectangle must fit within the square format, left to right. It can take any position top to bottom.

The two second largest rectangles must occupy either the two right columns or the two left columns. They can take any position top to bottom.

The three smallest rectangles may occupy any single column. They can take any position top to bottom.

This project is designed to present considerable potential for success. There are a number of reasons for this. First, the student is focused on selected issues throughout the project, and the decision-making process is directed toward these issues. Second, the square format serves to focus the student's attention on the elements and composition rather than on the proportion of a rectangular format. Third, a hierarchy of size exists and this hierarchy is present in the proportion of the elements. Since the grid is three columns wide, the length of all of the elements are in the proportion of 1:2:3. This proportion is pleasing and logical in a simple compositional structure, and is as important as all of the other visual theories in creating a cohesive composition.

The circle, too, is in proportion to the rectangular elements. It is approximately one-fourth of a unit in diameter and this diameter is roughly equivalent to the width of the longest rectangle.

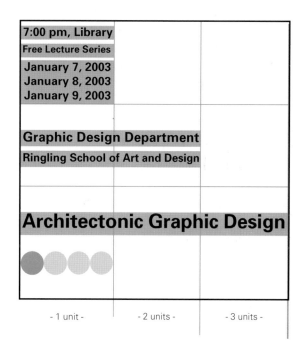

Grouping of elements is important in visual messages. Grouping permits an element to have an immediate visual relationship with another element in close proximity. Both similar and dissimilar elements can be grouped to create rhythm and repetition as well as larger areas of texture. The composition is simplified by grouping, white space, or negative space, is enhanced, and a stronger sense of visual order is created.

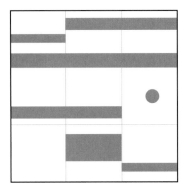

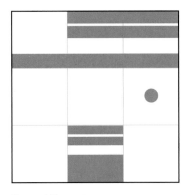

No Grouping
Without grouping of elements, the viewer has seven individual elements to visually absorb. The format appears unorganized and the elements too complex.

Grouped Elements
By grouping, the number of elements is reduced, which simplifies the composition and enhances the white space.

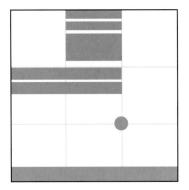

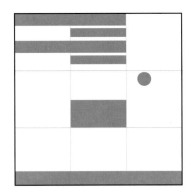

Grouping of Similar Elements
Rectangle elements of a similar width can be grouped.

Grouping of Dissimilar Elements
Rectangle elements of different widths can be grouped.

Negative space, or white space, is the space that is not occupied by the composition rectangles. The shape and composition of this space has a direct impact on how the composition will be perceived by the viewer. When elements are not grouped and each is surrounded by white space, the surrounding spaces are many and the composition appears chaotic and unorganized. As elements are grouped, the white spaces become fewer and larger, and a simplified, more cohesive perception of the composition is created.

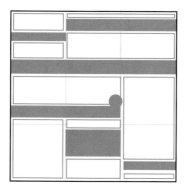

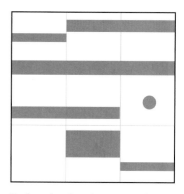

No Grouping: Complex Negative Spaces
In this ungrouped composition there are at least ten rectangles of negative space, as shown by the outlines, making the composition appear chaotic and visually uninviting.

No Grouping: Complex Negative Spaces

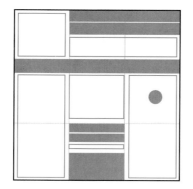

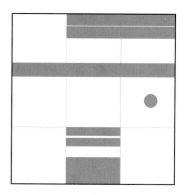

Grouped: Simple Negative Spaces
In this grouped composition there are six rectangles of negative space as shown by the outlines. These spaces are not only fewer in number but also larger and, therefore, more visually pleasing.

Grouped: Simple Negative Spaces

Perimeter Edge and Axial Relationships

Use of the perimeter edges of the format is critical in creating cohesive compositions. If none of the elements is near the top and bottom edges, as in the Perimeter Edge Relationships example below, the white space squeezes the elements, and the composition is ungrounded. When the elements of a composition move toward the top and bottom perimeter edges of a format, the white space is optimized, and the composition appears larger and more spacious by visual expansion.

Placement of elements within the grid structure creates axial alignments. When an axis occurs in the interior of the composition, strong visual relationships are formed that give the composition a sense of visual order. Axes on the left and right edges help to bring order to the composition but are considerably weaker visually. A single element does not create an axis; two or more elements create an axis, and, in general, the larger the number of aligned elements the stronger the axis.

Perimeter Edge Relationships

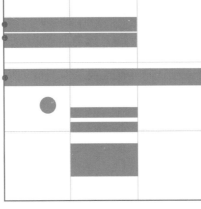

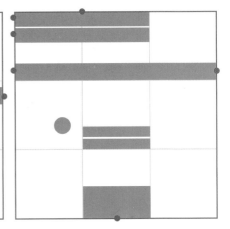

Weak Perimeter Edge Relationship
Since there are no elements touching the top or bottom edges, bars of inactivated white space squeeze the top and bottom of this composition.

Stronger Perimeter Edge Relationship
By allowing elements to touch all four sides of the format, all spaces are activated and the format expands visually.

Axial Relationships

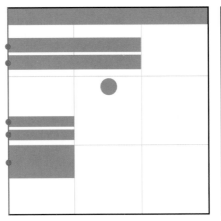

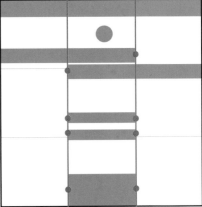

Weak Axial Relationship
The red line indicates the left edge axis in this composition. This relationship is weak because the interior alignments are minimal and the left edge position moves the eye off the page.

Stronger Axial Relationship
The interior axes in the center column are visually stronger because more elements align on each of these axes.

The 3 X 3 grid system corresponds to the rule of thirds that suggests when a rectangle or square is divided into thirds vertically and horizontally, the four intersecting points within the composition are the points of optimal focus. The designer uses placement and proximity to determine which of these points is hierarchically the most important.

An awareness of the law of thirds enables the designer to focus attention where it will most naturally occur and to control the compositional space. Elements do not need to land directly on the intersecting point as close proximity draws attention to them.

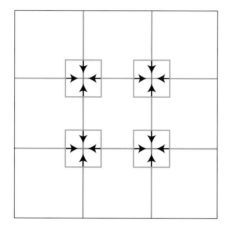

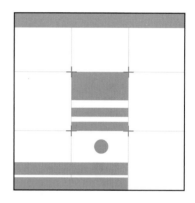

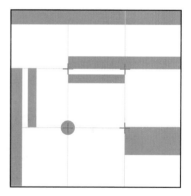

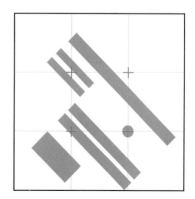

The Circle and Composition

As a wild-card element, the circle can be placed anywhere in the composition. As the circle nears lines of text it draws attention to them and modifies the lines. Placed in between lines of text, it separates and organizes the lines. Placed away from the text elements, it draws the eye and controls the visual flow during viewing, and has a tendency to balance the composition. Each different position changes the way the composition is viewed.

In all compositions the circle becomes an accent and an element that contrasts the rectangles. It can be a pivot point, an element of tension, a starting or stopping point, or it can contribute to visual organization or balance. It is a tool for the designer with which to consciously control the desired visual response.

Potential Circle Functions:
• Space Activator
• Pivot Point
• Tension
• Starting or Stopping Point
• Organization
• Balance

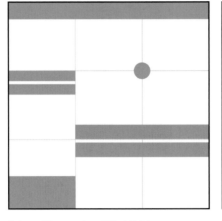

Balance Placement and Pivot Point
When the circle is placed in predictable alignment to the grid, a sense of visual balance is achieved. The circle is also a pivot point as the eye moves around the composition.

Space Activator
When the circle occupies a postion within a confined white space, the space becomes activated. A stronger sense of asymmetry is achieved in the composition as well as more visual interest.

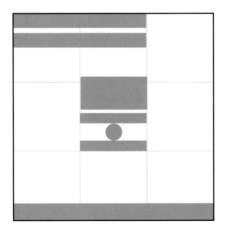

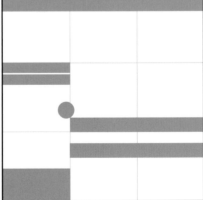

Tension
When the circle is placed very close to the other elements a visual tension occurs.

Tension
Placement of the circle near a 90º corner intensifies the contrast of shape and tension.

On this page all of the compositions are similar with only the placement of the circle changing. The black color of the circle calls attention to its position because its placement very clearly changes the way in which the viewers eye moves throughout the composition.

Placement of the circle near text often results in emphasis of that text. This emphasis changes the hierarchy as the circle becomes a starting point. Placement of the circle in between lines of text separates the lines and organizes them into individual groups, with a result of additional emphasis given to each line. Placing the circle so that it is surrounded by white space frequently causes the circle to become the pivot point. Trapping the circle tightly in between text and an edge results in both visual tension and an emphasis of the line of text.

Emphasis Placement and
Starting Point

Emphasis Placement and
Stopping Point

Emphasis and Tension Placement

Organization Placement

Emphasis and Organization
Placement

Organization Placement

Balance Placement

Balance Placement and
Pivot Point

Balance Placement

Horizontal Composition

The first in the series of exercises is the most simple—horizontal composition. Compositions are first developed in a series of small thumbnails as the visual principles of grouping, edge relationships, axial alignment, and circle placement are investigated. It is during the thumbnail phase that the visual principles begin to emerge.

A seemingly very simple task becomes more complex as the designer becomes increasingly aware of and sensitive to the nuances of composition. The initial compositions consist of the most obvious choices. Later evolutions of compositions are more interesting in that the designer begins to explore beyond the obvious.

The strongest compositions are refined in large scale, and, finally, lines of text are substituted for the rectangle elements. Those compositions that are the most ordered and compelling in the abstract version are also, invariably, the most interesting in the typographic version.

A visual hierarchy has already been built into this project by the assignment of each line of copy to the rectangles in the given grid structure. Further unity is achieved by employing a single face and weight of type for all lines in the composition. More than any other factor, the position of text and proximity of the circle will determine the hierarchy.

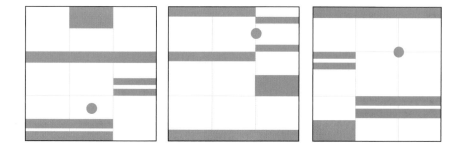

At the onset of the project, the student is inclined to create thumbnails rapidly and intuitively. This approach has its merits in that the most predictable solutions to visual organization are inevitably explored. However, there is a strong probability that one or more of the three approaches of top, bottom, and interior position of the longest rectangle will be overlooked. By organizing the project from the onset, attention can be knowingly focused on the three major approaches and to the key issues of composition within each approach.

The longest element, the rectangle that spans all three visual fields, controls the composition. Therefore, the three major approaches include: Long Rectangle in Top Position, Long Rectangle in Bottom Position, and Long Rectangle in Interior Position. The thumbnail compositions are divided into these three groups. In addition, each set of thumbnails will focus on specific compositional aspects of the project. The change of focus of each of the first two series provides the student a limited range of visual ideas to master. The third and final series brings all of the compositional aspects together.

Emphasis:
• Grouping
• Negative Space
• Perimeter Edge
• Axial Alignment
• The Law of Thirds
• Circle Placement
• Leading

Horizontal Composition

Series 1, Long Rectangle in Top Position
Emphasis: • Grouping
• Negative Space
• Perimeter Edge
• Axial Alignment

The primary focus is on the basic aspects of composition.

Series 2, Long Rectangle in Bottom Position
Emphasis: • The Law of Thirds
• Circle Placement
• Leading

The primary focus is on compositional control and enhancement.

Series 3, Long Rectangle in Interior Position
Emphasis: • Grouping
• Negative Space
• Perimeter Edge
• Axial Alignment
• The Law of Thirds
• Circle Placement
• Leading

This series brings all of the compositional aspects together.

Long Rectangle in Top Position
Thumbnails

The Long Rectangle in Top Position series of thumbnail compositions will use the longest rectangle only in the top position, touching the top of the format perimeter, or very near the top. Compositional emphasis is on grouping, negative space, perimeter edge, and axial alignment. Experimentation is encouraged as the student begins to understand which, and why, specific compositions are the most pleasing.

- **Grouping**
- **Negative Space**
- **Perimeter Edge**
- **Axial Alignment**
- The Law of Thirds
- Circle Placement
- Leading

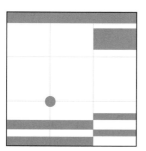 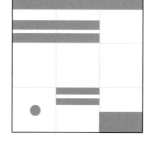 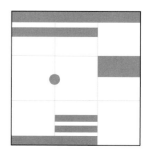

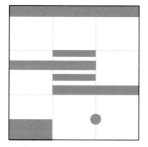 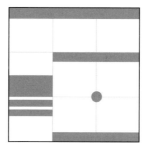 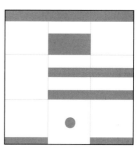

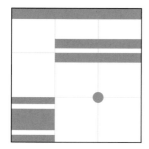 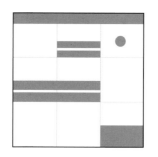 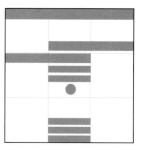

- **Grouping**
- **Negative Space**
- **Perimeter Edge**
- **Axial Alignment**
- The Law of Thirds
- Circle Placement
- Leading

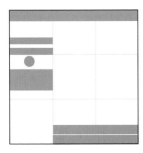

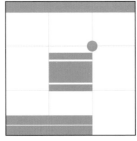

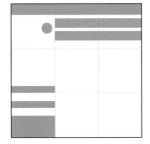

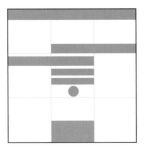

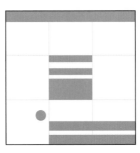

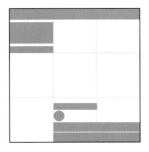

1. Critique (see next page)

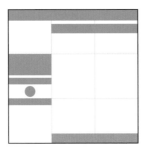

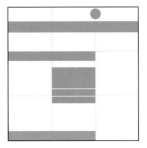

2. Critique (see next page)

- **Grouping**
- **Negative Space**
- **Perimeter Edge**
- **Axial Alignment**
- The Law of Thirds
- Circle Placement
- Leading

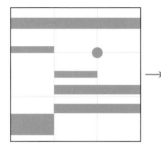

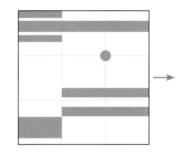

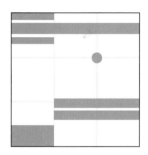

1. This work is less compositionally cohesive than many of the other thumbnails. There is trapped white space at the top that is inactivated, many elements are ungrouped causing the composition to feel complex, and the bottom edge of the perimeter is unused.

The white space at the top edge is activated by placing one of the narrow rectangles above it. A second narrow rectangle is grouped with the first by placing it under the long rectangle.

Finally, the two medium rectangles are grouped and leaded more tightly, and the thick rectangle is placed on the bottom edge to make the composition feel more spacious.

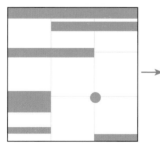

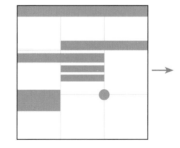

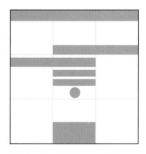

2. This work suffers from some of the same problems as the work above. Elements need to be grouped more tightly to simplify the composition, and the interior axial alignments need to be strengthened.

The two midsize rectangles remain offset. However, they are more tightly leaded and are grouped with the two small rectangles.

Finally, the thick rectangle is placed on the bottom edge of the perimeter to anchor the composition, and the circle is placed in the center to modify the strong axial alignments on the center column.

Text Adjustments
Lines of text replace
the gray rectangles in
the strongest thumbnail
compositions. Fine
tuning adjustments are
made to the text leading
in the final compositions.

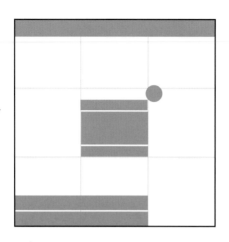

Architectonic Graphic Design

Free Lecture Series
January 7, 2003
January 8, 2003
January 9, 2003
7:00 pm, Library

Graphic Design Department

Ringling School of Art and Design

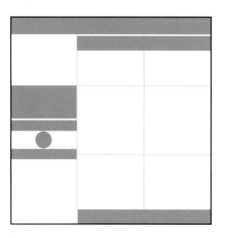

Architectonic Graphic Design
Graphic Design Department

January 7, 2003
January 8, 2003
January 9, 2003
Free Lecture Series

7:00 pm, Library

Ringling School of Art and Design

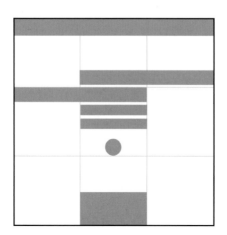

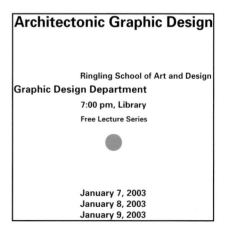

Architectonic Graphic Design

Ringling School of Art and Design
Graphic Design Department
7:00 pm, Library
Free Lecture Series

January 7, 2003
January 8, 2003
January 9, 2003

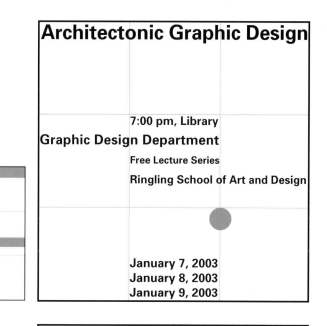

Architectonic Graphic Design

7:00 pm, Library

Graphic Design Department

Free Lecture Series

Ringling School of Art and Design

January 7, 2003
January 8, 2003
January 9, 2003

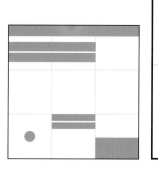

Architectonic Graphic Design

Graphic Design Department

Ringling School of Art and Design

7:00 pm, Library

Free Lecture Series

January 7, 2003
January 8, 2003
January 9, 2003

The bottom position is the most stable compositional place-ment for the long rectangle and gives stability to all of the other elements. This is as if gravity was at work causing the longest or heaviest element to fall to the bottom. The other composi-tional elements can be moved freely in the space above because stability already exists below.

- Grouping
- Negative Space
- Perimeter Edge
- Axial Alignment
- **The Law of Thirds**
- **Circle Placement**
- **Leading**

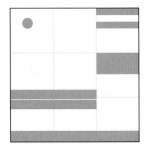
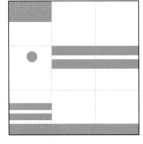
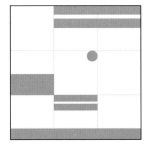

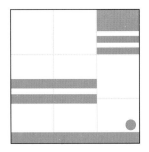
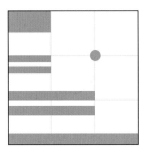
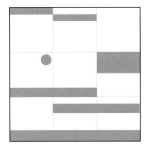

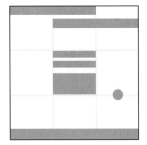
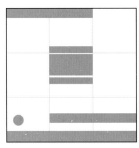
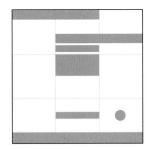

- Grouping
- Negative Space
- Perimeter Edge
- Axial Alignment
- **The Law of Thirds**
- **Circle Placement**
- **Leading**

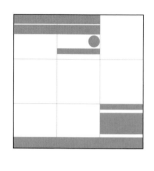 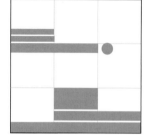 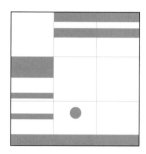

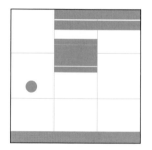 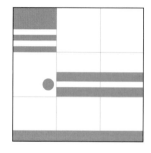 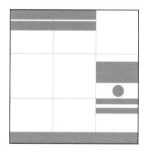

1. Critique (see next page)

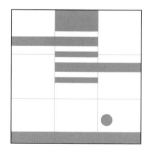 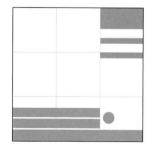 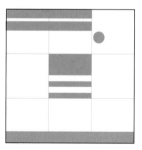

2. Critique (see next page)

- Grouping
- Negative Space
- Perimeter Edge
- Axial Alignment
- **The Law of Thirds**
- **Circle Placement**
- **Leading**

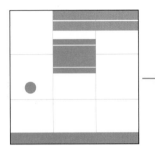

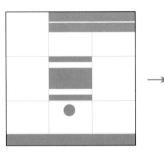

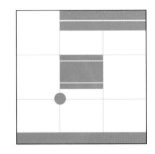

1. This work is fairly compositionally cohesive. The next two revisions consciously employ the law of thirds to investigate the possibility of a more cohesive composition.

The law of thirds suggests that when a rectangle or square is divided into thirds vertically and horizontally the four intersecting points within the composition are the points of optimal focus.

The two variations investigate the results of a change in leading and a change in placement of the circle.

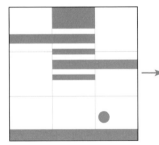

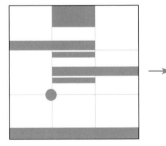

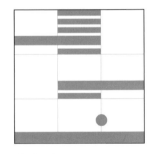

2. This work is also fairly compositionally cohesive. The next two revisions consciously employ variations in leading to investigate the possibility of a more cohesive composition.

Tightening the leading creates two distinct groups of dissimilar elements.

Moving the groups apart makes them more distinct. The breaking of the thick rectangle into three lines creates a different rhythm.

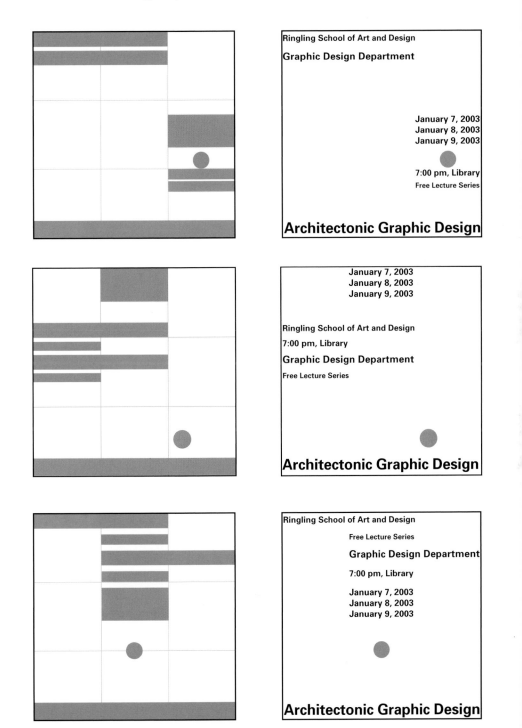

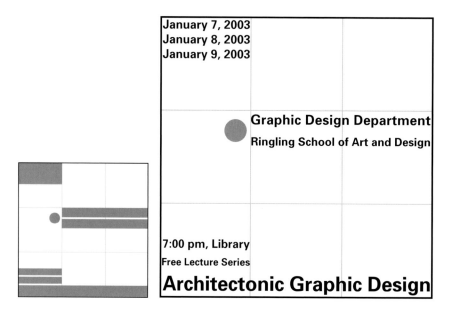

January 7, 2003
January 8, 2003
January 9, 2003

Graphic Design Department

Ringling School of Art and Design

7:00 pm, Library

Free Lecture Series

Architectonic Graphic Design

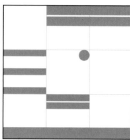

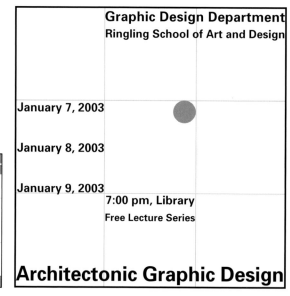

Graphic Design Department
Ringling School of Art and Design

January 7, 2003

January 8, 2003

January 9, 2003

7:00 pm, Library

Free Lecture Series

Architectonic Graphic Design

The interior position is a precarious one for the long rectangle. Because it spans the width of the format, it divides the square into two smaller rectangles. If no elements are placed in one of the rectangular divisions, that space is inactivated and visually uncomfortable. The placement of at least one element in each of the rectangular divisions activates the total space.

The placement of the longest rectangle in the interior creates an aesthetic disadvantage. This is the result of dividing a harmonious square format into two less harmonious rectangles. Even with both spaces activated, the result is decidedly less pleasing than compositions that are not divided by the long rectangle.

Long Rectangle in Interior Position
Thumbnails

- **Grouping**
- **Negative Space**
- **Perimeter Edge**
- **Axial Alignment**
- **The Law of Thirds**
- **Circle Placement**
- **Leading**

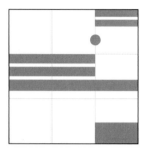

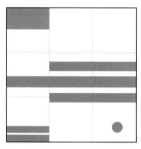

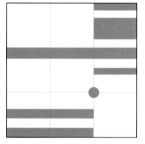

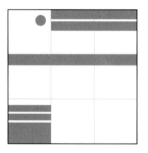

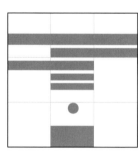

1. Critique (see next page)

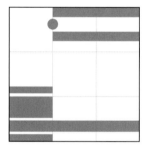

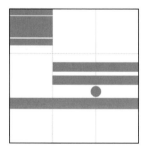

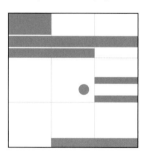

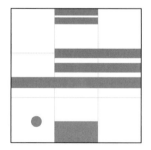

2. Critique (see next page)

- **Grouping**
- **Negative Space**
- **Perimeter Edge**
- **Axial Alignment**
- **The Law of Thirds**
- **Circle Placement**
- **Leading**

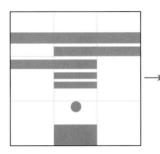 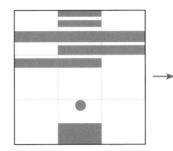 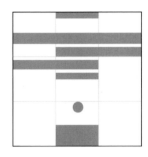

1. The composition has good interior alignment but the long rectangle has isolated an inactivated space at the top. This white space is awkward and makes the composition feel as if the elements are bottom heavy.

Since the rhythm and repetition of the small and medium rectangles are interesting, the small rectangles are moved up as space activators.

A single element, such as a small rectangle, can also activate the space. As an isolated element, it will attract considerable attention.

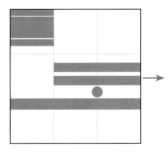 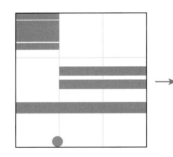 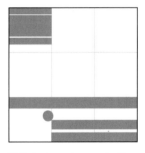

2. Similar to the work above, this composition has trapped inactivated white space. This white space is awkward and makes the composition feel as if the elements are floating toward the top.

A single element, in this case the circle, is enough to activate the white space and anchor the composition.

Multiple elements are activating the white space, and the circle creates tension and attracts attention.

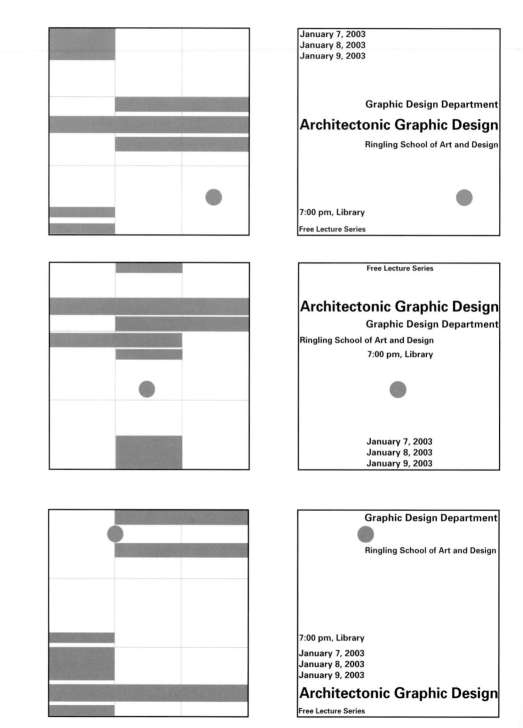

January 7, 2003
January 8, 2003
January 9, 2003

Graphic Design Department
Architectonic Graphic Design
Ringling School of Art and Design

7:00 pm, Library
Free Lecture Series

Free Lecture Series

Architectonic Graphic Design
Graphic Design Department
Ringling School of Art and Design
7:00 pm, Library

January 7, 2003
January 8, 2003
January 9, 2003

Graphic Design Department
Ringling School of Art and Design

7:00 pm, Library
January 7, 2003
January 8, 2003
January 9, 2003
Architectonic Graphic Design
Free Lecture Series

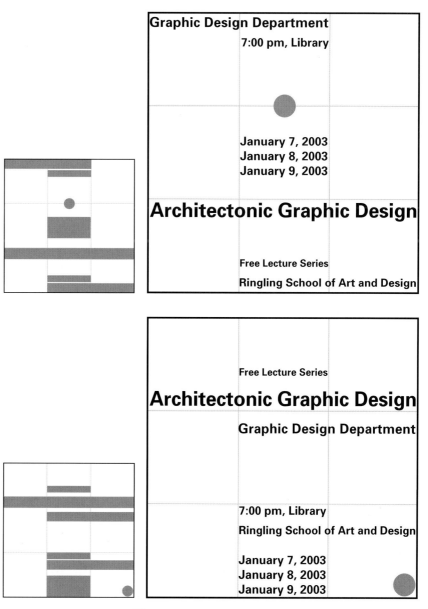

Graphic Design Department

7:00 pm, Library

January 7, 2003
January 8, 2003
January 9, 2003

Architectonic Graphic Design

Free Lecture Series

Ringling School of Art and Design

Free Lecture Series

Architectonic Graphic Design

Graphic Design Department

7:00 pm, Library

Ringling School of Art and Design

January 7, 2003
January 8, 2003
January 9, 2003

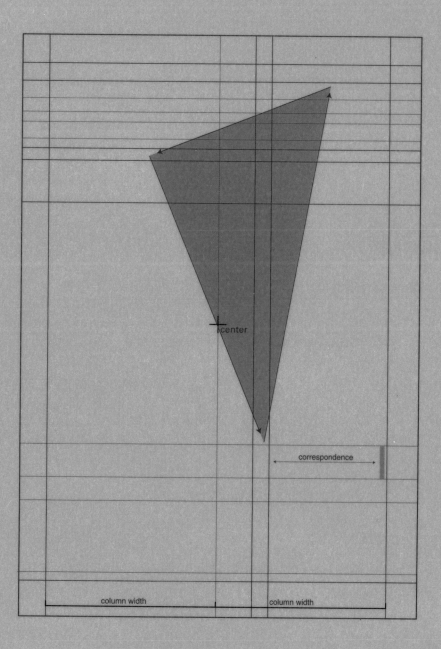

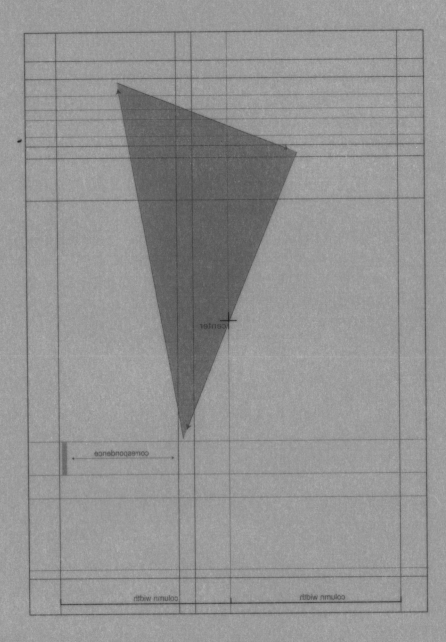

correspondence

center

column width   column width

Jan Tschichold, at the young age of twenty-three, wrote a special issue of a printing trade journal entitled *Elementare Typographie*. Through this journal Tschichold introduced his philosophy and the work and ideas of El Lissitzky to the professional world. In 1928 the book *Die Neue Typographie: The New Typography* was published and became an influential milestone of communication design. This book analyzed typographic design, attempted to systematize the "new typography," and advocated asymmetric composition with negative space and leading as important elements to the underlying structure.

The brochure for *Die Neue Typographie*, shown below, embodies the principles set forth by Tschichold and is a study in subtle contrast. The type is an unembellished sans serif set in a two-column overlapping grid. The columns are the same width as shown on the overlay and overlap to create a narrower right column with a shorter bold column near the bottom.

VORZUGS-ANGEBOT

Im VERLAG DES BILDUNGSVERBANDES der Deutschen Buchdrucker, Berlin SW 61, Dreibundstr. 5, erscheint demnächst:

JAN TSCHICHOLD
Lehrer an der Meisterschule für Deutschlands Buchdrucker in München

DIE NEUE TYPOGRAPHIE

**Handbuch für die gesamte Fachwelt
und die drucksachenverbrauchenden Kreise**

Das Problem der neuen gestaltenden Typographie hat eine lebhafte Diskussion bei allen Beteiligten hervorgerufen. Wir glauben dem Bedürfnis, die aufgeworfenen Fragen ausführlich behandelt zu sehen, zu entsprechen, wenn wir jetzt ein Handbuch der **NEUEN TYPOGRAPHIE** herausbringen.

Es kam dem Verfasser, einem ihrer bekanntesten Vertreter, in diesem Buche zunächst darauf an, den engen Zusammenhang der neuen Typographie mit dem **Gesamtkomplex heutigen Lebens** aufzuzeigen und zu beweisen, daß die neue Typographie ein ebenso notwendiger Ausdruck einer neuen Gesinnung ist wie die neue Baukunst und alles Neue, das mit unserer Zeit anbricht. Diese geschichtliche Notwendigkeit der neuen Typographie belegt weiterhin eine kritische Darstellung der **alten Typographie**. Die Entwicklung der **neuen Malerei**, die für alles Neue unserer Zeit geistig bahnbrechend gewesen ist, wird in einem reich illustrierten Aufsatz des Buches leicht faßlich dargestellt. Ein kurzer Abschnitt „**Zur Geschichte der neuen Typographie**" leitet zu dem wichtigsten Teile des Buches, den **Grundbegriffen der neuen Typographie** über. Diese werden klar herausgeschält, richtige und falsche Beispiele einander gegenübergestellt. Zwei weitere Artikel behandeln „**Photographie und Typographie**" und „**Neue Typographie und Normung**".

Der Hauptwert des Buches für den Praktiker besteht in dem zweiten Teil „**Typographische Hauptformen**" (siehe das nebenstehende Inhaltsverzeichnis). Es fehlte bisher an einem Werke, das wie dieses Buch die schon bei einfachen Satzaufgaben auftauchenden gestalterischen Fragen in gebührender Ausführlichkeit behandelte. Jeder Teilabschnitt enthält neben **allgemeinen typographischen Regeln** vor allem die Abbildungen aller in Betracht kommenden **Normblätter** des Deutschen Normenausschusses, alle andern (z. B. postalischen) **Vorschriften** und zahlreiche Beispiele, Gegenbeispiele und Schemen.

Für jeden Buchdrucker, insbesondere jeden Akzidenzsetzer, wird „Die neue Typographie" ein **unentbehrliches Handbuch** sein. Von nicht geringerer Bedeutung ist es für Reklamefachleute, Gebrauchsgraphiker, Kaufleute, Photographen, Architekten, Ingenieure und Schriftsteller, also für alle, die mit dem Buchdruck in Berührung kommen.

INHALT DES BUCHES

Werden und Wesen der neuen Typographie
Das neue Weltbild
Die alte Typographie (Rückblick und Kritik)
Die neue Kunst
Zur Geschichte der neuen Typographie
Die Grundbegriffe der neuen Typographie
Photographie und Typographie
Neue Typographie und Normung

Typographische Hauptformen
Das Typosignet
Der Geschäftsbrief
Der Halbbrief
Briefhüllen ohne Fenster
Fensterbriefhüllen
Die Postkarte
Die Postkarte mit Klappe
Die Geschäftskarte
Die Besuchskarte
Werbsachen (Karten, Blätter, Prospekte, Kataloge)
Das Typoplakat
Das Bildplakat
Schildformate, Tafeln und Rahmen
Inserate
Die Zeitschrift
Die Tageszeitung
Die illustrierte Zeitung
Tabellensatz
Das neue Buch

Bibliographie
Verzeichnis der Abbildungen
Register

typ. tschichold

Das Buch enthält über **125 Abbildungen,** von denen etwa ein Viertel **zweifarbig** gedruckt ist, und umfaßt gegen **200** Seiten auf gutem Kunstdruckpapier. Es erscheint im Format DIN A5 (148× 210 mm) und ist biegsam in Ganzleinen gebunden.

. **Preis** bei Vorbestellung bis 1. Juni 1928:   **5.00** RM
durch den Buchhandel nur zum Preise von   **6.50** RM

Bestellschein umstehend ■▶

Jan Tschichold, 1928

El Lissitzky was closely tied to the Bauhaus and the Bauhaus masters, including Jan Tschichold, László Moholy-Nagy, and Theo van Doesburg. He was a prolific writer, lectured widely, and is credited with inspiring a generation of typographic experimentation. He pioneered the experimental exploitation of the letterpress type case by using rules, space bars, and ornaments as elements of composition and images.

The pages from *The Isms of Art* represent an approach to a complex communication problem of designing a book in three languages. Lissitzky chose to use a highly structured grid system of columns and heavy rules, which function as elements of organization and emphasis. In addition, the rules were true to the constructivist and the suprematist movements in art and design that focused on nonrepresentational geometry and primary color as pure communication. The horizontal versus vertical stress of the heavy rules becomes the unifying device that organizes the information.

Title Page (above)
The organizational system on the title page is a horizontal system that divides the page into three visual fields, and the visual stress is horizontal.

Text Page (right)
Conversely, the organizational system on the text page is a vertical system that divides the page into three vertical columns. The horizontal divisions still exist; the page is horizontally divided to separate the introduction by Malewitsch, and sections on cubism, futurism, and expressionism.

El Lissitzky, 1923

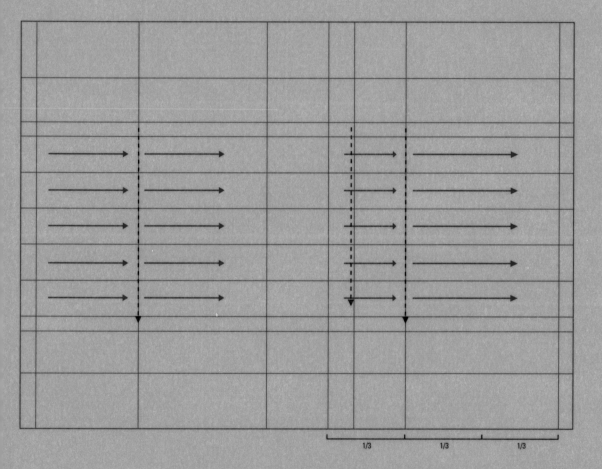

1/3   1/3   1/3

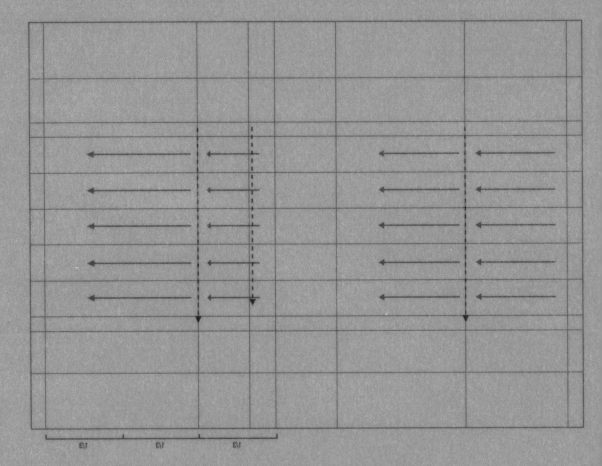

Spread from the Catalog of Bauhaus Products

Herbert Bayer was a student at the original Bauhaus in Thuringia, Germany, in 1921, where he studied under Wassily Kandinsky and, later, under László Moholy-Nagy. By 1925, along with former students Marcel Breuer, Joost Schmidt, and Joseph Albers, he was appointed a teacher at the new Bauhaus in Dessau. Strongly influenced by the "isms" of the time, he was even more inspired by the functional and rational approach to typography of the Bauhaus.

Bayer's design for the Bauhaus catalog reveals a sensitive approach to the use of nonobjective elements. The change in weight of the rules from extremely heavy to hairlines is a beautiful contrast. Rhythm and repetition play an important role as shapes are repeated to create both a visual organization of the text groups and a strong vertical stress that carries the eye down the page. Each page of the spread shown below ends with a heavy nonobjective element—a heavy horizontal rule on the left and a circle on the right.

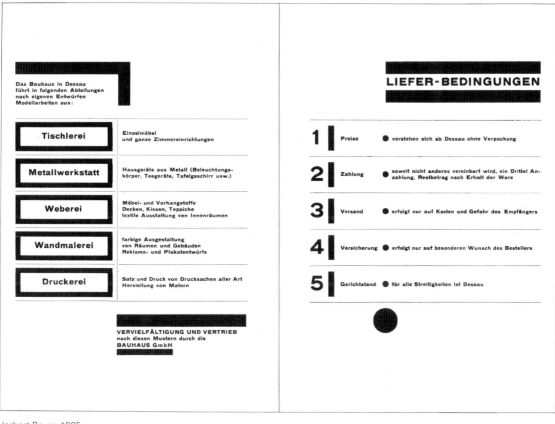

Herbert Bayer, 1925

Below is the "before" version of the Theatre Am Hechtplatz patron list. On this page each patron has a small advertisement with a logo and descriptive text, resulting in a confusing, overwhelming page. On the "after" page (opposite page) a design system has been created that consolidates the information typographically. Each advertisement is separated and organized by a rule, and the descriptive text is organized through a common font and systemized placement of text.

The structure is defined as eight columns by twelve square visual fields. This structure is divided into one-third and two-thirds, with the top third holding the title and text and the bottom two-thirds holding the patron advertisements. The very top row of visual fields is reserved for the title. Each patron has either a four-column by four-visual-field space or a four-column by eight-visual-field space.

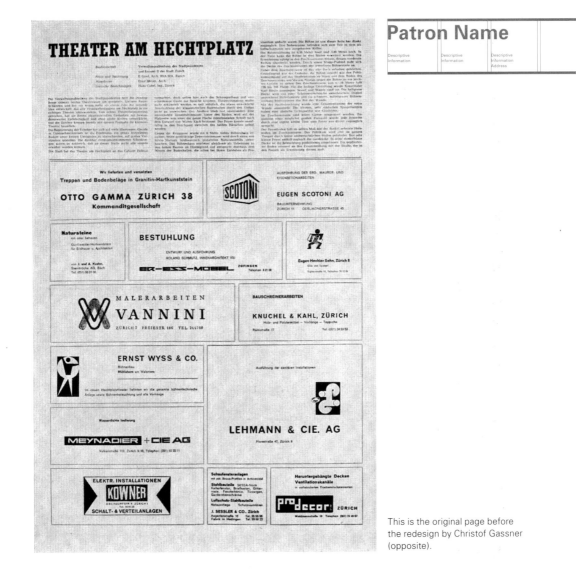

This is the original page before the redesign by Christof Gassner (opposite).

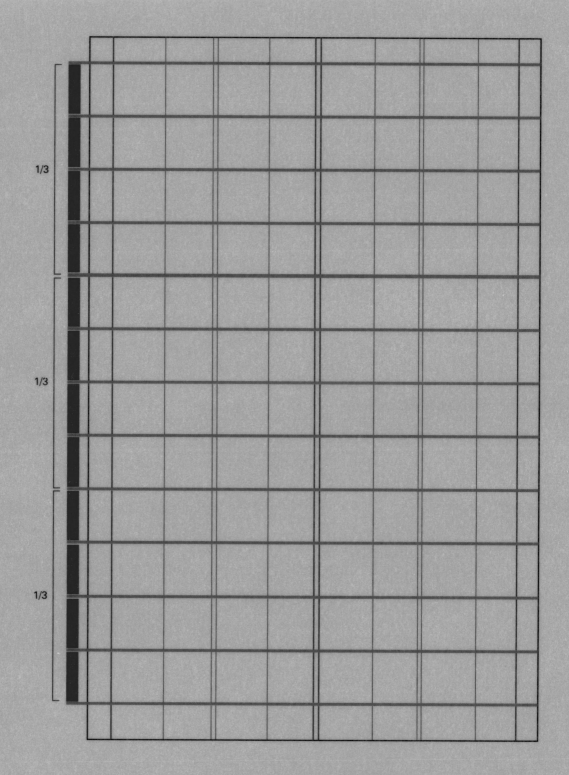

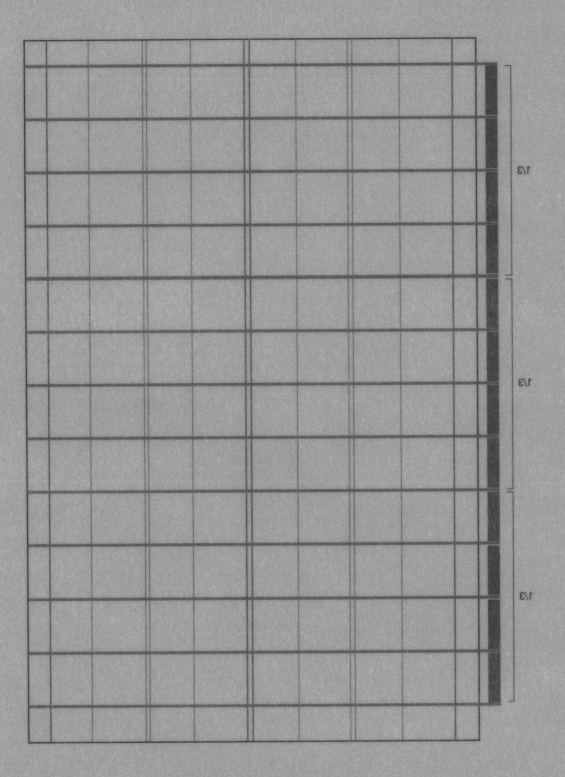

Theater am Hechtplatz

Sie hat 60 Ze	der halbfetten Akzid	Dies ist ein Schriftmuster der halbfetten	auf zehn Zentimeter. Dies ist ein Schrift	ein Schriftmuster der halbfetten Akzidenz
	auf	Sie hat 60 Zeichen auf 10 Zentimeter. Die	zwei Punkt durchschossen. Sie hat	hat 60 Zeichen auf zehn Zentimeter. Dies
	zwei Punkt durch	8 Punkt, hier mit zwei Punkt durch	grotesk acht Punkt, hier mit zwei Punkt	Punkt, hier mit zwei Punkt durchschossen.
Ichen auf 10 Zentim	grotesk acht	ein Schriftmuster der halbfetten Akzidenz	Akzidenzgrotesk acht Punkt, hier mit zwei	ist ein Schriftmuster der Akzidenzgrotesk
	Akziden	hat 60 Zeichen auf zehn Zentimeter. Dies	Zentimeter. Dies ist die halbfette	60 Zeichen auf zehn Zentimeter. Dies ist
	zehn Zentimeter. Di	ist ein Schriftmuster der Akzidenzgrotesk	schossen. Sie hat 60 Zeichen auf zehn	der halbfetten Akzidenzgrotesk acht Punkt
	schoss	Punkt, hier mit zwei Punkt durchschossen.	mit zwei Punkt durchschossen. Sie hat 60	auf zehn Zentimeter. Dies ist ein Schrift
der halbfett	mit zwei Pu	60 Zeichen auf zehn Zentimeter. Dies ist	der Akzidenzgrotesk acht Punkt, hier mit	zwei Punkt durchschossen. Sie hat 60
	der Akzid	mit zwei Punkt durchschossen. Sie hat	Dies ist ein Schriftmuster der halbfetten	grotesk echt Punkt, hier mit zwei Punkt
kzidenzgrotesk acht	Dies ist ei	der halbfetten Akzidenzgrotesk acht Punkt	Sie hat 60 Zeichen auf 10 Zentimeter.	zehn Zentimeter. Dies ist die halbfette
	Sie hat 60 Zeich	auf zehn Zentimeter. Dies ist ein Schrift	ein Schriftmuster der halbfetten Akzidenz	schossen. Sie hat 60 Zeichen auf zehn
		zwei Punkt durchschossen. Sie hat	hat 60 Zeichen auf zehn Zentimeter. Dies	der Akzidenzgrotesk acht Punkt, hier mit
		grotesk acht Punkt, hier mit zwei Punkt	Punkt, hier mit zwei Punkt durchschossen.	mit zwei Punkt durchschossen. Sie hat 60
		Akzidenzgrotesk acht Punkt, hier mit zwei	ist ein Schriftmuster der Akzidenzgrotesk	der Akzidenzgrotesk acht Punkt, hier mit
		mit zwei Punkt durchschossen. Sie hat 60	60 Zeichen auf zehn Zentimeter. Dies ist	Dies ist ein Schriftmuster der halbfetten
		der Akzidenzgrotesk acht Punkt, hier mit	der halbfetten Akzidenzgrotesk acht Punkt	8 Punkt, hier mit zwei Punkt durch
		Dies ist ein Schriftmuster der halbfetten	auf zehn Zentimeter. Dies ist ein Schrift	ein Schriftmuster der halbfetten Akzidenz
		Sie hat 60 Zeichen auf 10 Zentimeter.	zwei Punkt durchschossen. Sie hat	hat 60 Zeichen auf zehn Zentimeter. Dies
		9 Punkt, hier mit zwei Punkt durch	grotesk acht Punkt, hier mit zwei Punkt	Punkt, hier mit zwei Punkt durchschossen.
		ein Schriftmuster der halbfetten Akzidenz	zehn Zentimeter. Dies ist die halbfette	ist ein Schriftmuster der Akzidenzgrotesk
		Punkt, hier mit zwei Punkt durchschossen.	schossen. Sie hat 60 Zeichen auf zehn	60 Zeichen auf zehn Zentimeter. Dies ist
		ist ein Schriftmuster der Akzidenzgrotesk	mit zwei Punkt durchschossen. Sie hat 60	mit zwei Punkt durchschossen. Sie hat 60
		60 Zeichen auf zehn Zentimeter. Dies	der Akzidenzgrotesk acht Punkt, hier mit	
		mit zwei Punkt durchschossen. Sie hat 60	Dies ist ein Schriftmuster der halbfetten	

Eugen Scotoni AG

ie hat sechzig	8 Punkt, hier mi
k acht Punkt, hier	ein Schriftmuster de
	hat 60 Ze

J. & A. Kuster

Zeichen auf	Dies ist ein Sc
	Sie h
	8 Punkt, hier mit

Kowner

zgrotesk 8	ein Schriftm	Dies ist ein Schr
in Schriftmuste	hat 60 Zeichen	Sie hat 6
		8 Punkt, hier mit

Knuchel & Kahl

zehn Zentimeter. Di	Punkt, hier mit	mit zwei Punkt
	ist ei	der halb
	60 Zeichen auf ze	

Eugen Hechler Sohn

halbfetten Akzid	auf zehn Zentime
	zwei Punkt durch

Vannini

Otto Gamma

grotesk	Punkt, hier mit zwei
Akzidenzgrotesk	ist ein S
	60 Zeichen auf z

Lehmann & Cie. AG

hriftmuster de	8 Punkt, hier mi
	ein Schr
	hat 60 Zeichen a

Ernst Wyss & Co.

Akzidenzg	iltmuster der halbfe

Sessler & Co.

Punkt, hier mit zwei	60 Zeichen	Punkt, hier mit zwe	mit zwei Punkt dur
ist ein Schri	mit zwei Punk	ist ein	der halbfetten Ak
		60 Zeichen auf ze	

Meynadier & Cie. AG

ER ESS Möbel

mit zwei	8 Punkt, hier mi
der halbfetten	ein Schr
	hat 60 Zeichen au

Prodecor AG

der halbfe	zwei Punkt durche
auf zehn Zen	grotesk ach
	Akzidenzgrotesk a

der Akzidenzgrote	zehn Zentimeter	durchschos	ist ein Schriftmuster	8 Punkt
Dies is	schossen		60 Zeichen auf	ein Schriftmuster
Sie hat 60 Zeich	mit zwei Punkt dur		mit zwei Punkt dur	

Christof Gassner,
c. 1960

The SamataMason Web Site structure is extremely flexible and permits a wide range of variety. Central to the structure is a horizontal axis that holds the text, icon, and the firm's motto, "We do good work for good people." In addition, this axis holds the user's navigational controls for viewing supplementary images. Images and text can appear above or below the axis in either a square or rectangular format.

The warm-gray background allows text and images to be highlighted in either white or black, again giving flexibility in content organization and the way the site is read. This gives order to the space and directs the user's attention where intended. The images are splashes of color that attract the viewer's eye.

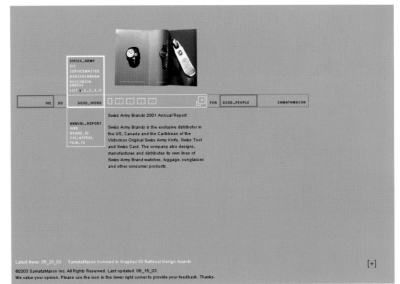

Design Firm
SamataMason, Dundee, Illinois

Art Directors and Designers
Dave Mason, Kevin Krueger,
2001

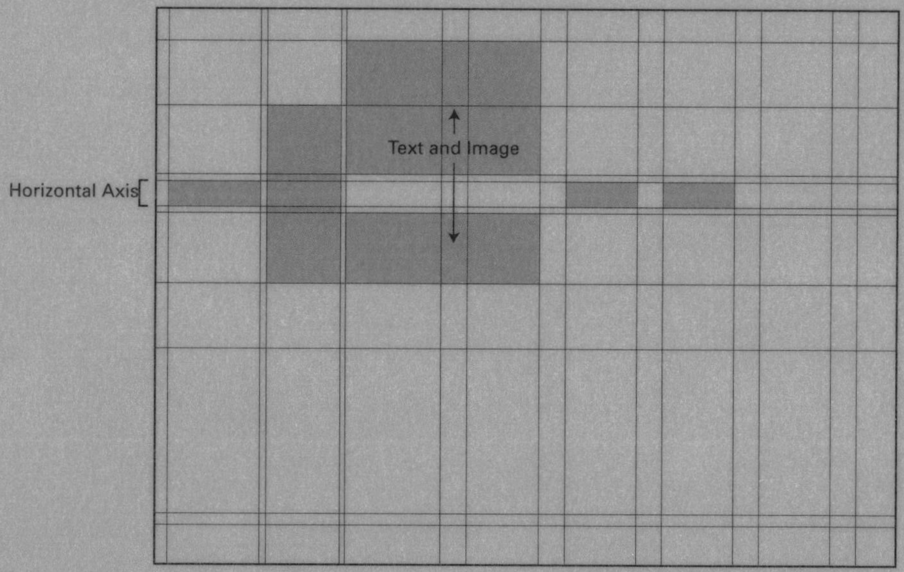

Horizontal Axis

Text and Image

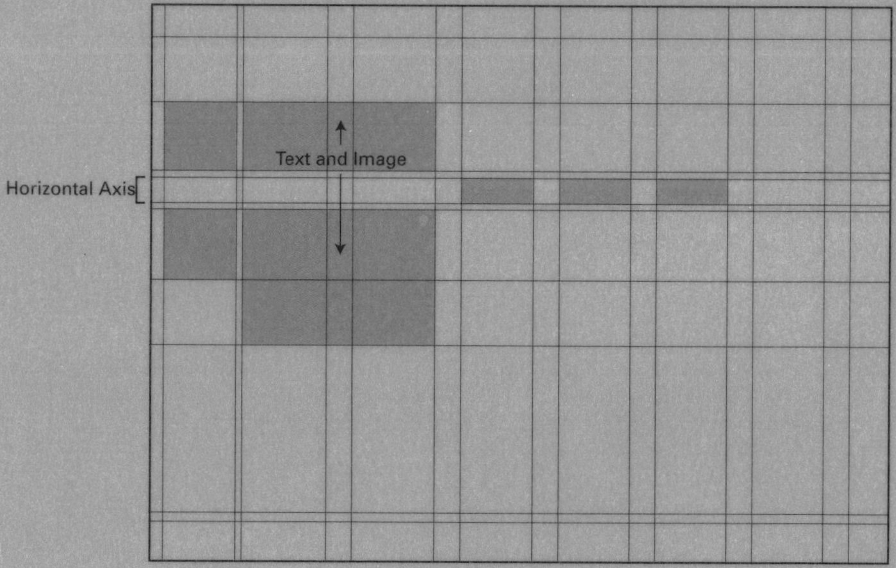

Horizontal Axis

Text and Image

Text and Image

Horizontal Axis

Text and Image

Horizontal Axis

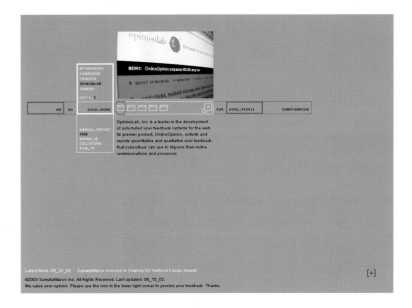

OpinionLab, Inc. is a leader in the development of automated user feedback systems for the web. Its premier product, OnlineOpinion, collects and reports quantitative and qualitative user feedback that subscribers can use to improve their online communications and processes.

SamataMason's principal office is in a converted bowling alley on the banks of the Fox River in West Dundee, Illinois (a suburb of Chicago).

A second office is located in a harbor front loft in Vancouver, BC.

289_ALEXANDER
SUITE_501
VANCOUVER_BC
V6A_4H8
CANADA
P_604.684.6060
F_604.684.4274

These are two of a series of posters for the Institute for Architecture and Urban Studies (IAUS). The posters promote changing lectures and exhibitions on a variety of topics. Since the topics changed dramatically, the design system became an identity for the IAUS during 1979 and 1980 and allowed for variations within the structure.

The structure consists of four main columns subdivided to create eight vertical columns and eight horizontal square visual fields.

The rows of visual fields are separated by a black rule about the same width as the column gutter. The top two visual fields are reserved for the heavy black rule, name and address, and a large red title of the newest exhibition. The next row of visual fields contains the main information in red text above and below a black separation rule. The row of visual fields just above the center is reserved for a horizontal band of images. The four rows of visual fields below the center contain descriptive text with the option of an image, as in the Austrian Architecture poster below.

Vignelli and Associates, 1979–80

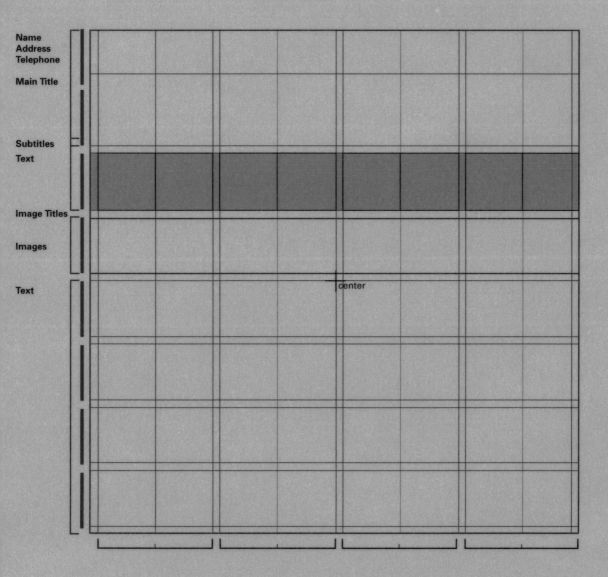

Name
Address
Telephone

Main Title

Subtitles

Text

Image Titles

Images

Text

center

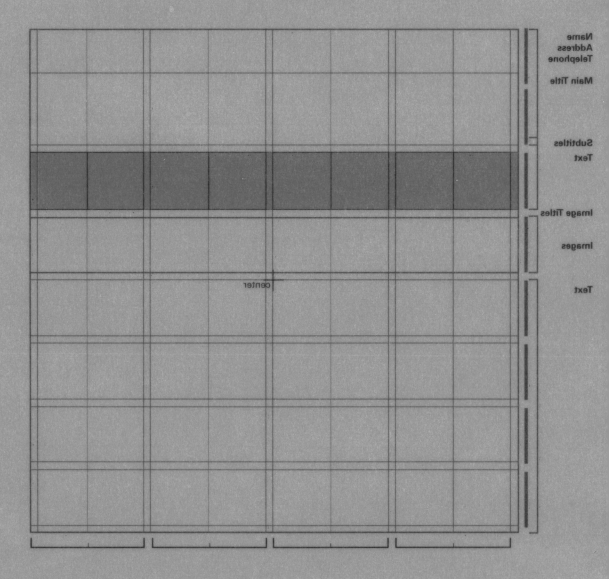

Name
Address
Telephone

Main Title

Subtitles

Text

Image Titles

Images

Text

center

The posters use an economy of means by employing only two ink colors, red and black, that appear all the richer by the use of a duotone in the images. Economy is also present in the design system that enables the viewer to fluidly move from titles to text to images and readily access information.

43

Sotheby's is one of the largest auction houses in the world, with two New York City galleries on Madison Avenue and York Avenue. The Sotheby's advertisement system needed to be flexible and highly informative because the wide variety of auction merchandise changed weekly. With the design system in place, templates could be used to quickly change the information while retaining the systemized look of the advertisements.

The distinct and beautifully controlled hierarchy of information allows the viewer to see, at a glance, what will be auctioned that week at both galleries. The system fluidly moves from the most general information, the auction title and image, to the most specific, when and where the auction is held. The bold black horizontal rules emphasize the title, Sotheby's, and clearly separate and organize the categories of merchandise.

Fine Art Auctioneers   Since 1744

SOTHEBY'S

Madison Avenue Galleries
980 Madison Avenue.
New York 10021
(212) 472-3400

York Avenue Galleries
1334 York Avenue.
New York 10021
(212) 472-3400

Exhibition Galleries open Monday through Saturday 10 to 5. Sundays 1 to 5. Tuesday evenings until 7:30. All property on view until 3 pm the day prior to sale. No Jewelry, Stamp or Coin exhibitions on Sundays or Tuesday evenings.

Catalogues available at both galleries and may be ordered by mail. Request by sale number and enclose check to Sotheby's. Dept. NYC, 980 Madison Avenue, New York 10021. For further information, please contact the Subscription Department (212) 472-3414.

Madison Avenue Galleries

Fine Jewelry

Auction: Wednesday, March 18 at 2 pm.

Exhibition: Saturday, Monday, and Tuesday, March 14, 16 and 17 from 10 am to 4:45 pm and Wednesday, March 18 from 10 am to 12 noon. (Note: No Sunday or Tuesday evening exhibitions.)

Illustrated catalogue S8, S10 by mail. Order by sale no. 4566M.

Shown: Pair of eighteen-karat gold and enamel earclips, signed Webb. (lot 115)

Madison Avenue Galleries

Old Master Paintings

Auction: Thursday, March 19 at 2 pm.

Exhibition: Saturday, March 14 through Wednesday, March 18.

Illustrated catalogue S7, S8 by mail. Order by sale no. 4567M.

Shown: Richard Cosway, R.A., *Portrait of a Gentleman in a Landscape*, oval, oil on canvas, 29½ x 24½ inches. (lot 154)

York Avenue Galleries

Decorative Works of Art, Furniture and Rugs

Auction: Thursday, March 19 at 10:15 am (continuing all day) and Friday, March 20 at 10:15 am and 2 pm.

Exhibition: Saturday, March 14 through noon on day prior to date of sale.

Lecture: Sunday, March 15 at 2 pm in conjunction with this exhibition.

Catalogue S4, S5 by mail. Order by sale no. 4568Y.

Shown: Le verre francais cameo glass vase, etched signature, height 13 inches. (lot 105)

York Avenue Galleries

Decorative Works of Art

Auction: Thursday, March 26 at 10:15 am (continuing all day).

Exhibition: Saturday, March 21 through noon on Wednesday, March 25.

Lecture: Sunday, March 22 at 2 pm in conjunction with this exhibition.

Catalogue S4, S5 by mail. Order by sale no. 4569Y.

Shown: Chinese porcelain bottle-form vase, height 15½ inches. (lot 543)

Los Angeles Galleries

Highly Important Jewelry

Auction: Tuesday, March 31 at 1:30 pm and 7:30 pm.

Exhibition: Friday, March 27 through Sunday, March 29 from noon to 5 pm each day.

Illustrated catalogue S7, S9 by mail. Order by sale no. 301 with check enclosed to Sotheby's Los Angeles, 7660 Beverly Blvd, Los Angeles, California 90036. Catalogues also available at our New York Galleries.

Inquiries: Mr. Joseph Gill, (213) 937-5130, ext. 31.

Shown: Russian eighteen-karat yellow gold enamel and diamond presentation box. (lot 315)

Fine Art Auctioneers   Since 1744

SOTHEBY'S

Madison Avenue Galleries
980 Madison Avenue.
New York 10021
(212) 472-3400

York Avenue Galleries
1331 York Avenue.
New York 10021
(212) 472.3400

Exhibition Galleries open Monday through Saturday 10 to 5. Sundays 1 to 5. Tuesday evenings until 7:30. All property on view until 3 pm the day prior to sale. No Jewelry, Stamp or Coin exhibitions on Sundays or Tuesday evenings.

Catalogues available at both galleries or by mail. Request by sale number and enclose check to Sotheby's. Dept. NYC, 980 Madison Avenue. New York 10021. For further information, please contact the Subscription Department (212) 472.3414.

York Avenue Galleries

Decorative Works of Art, Judaica, Furniture & Rugs

Japanese Prints

Auction: Friday, January 16 at 10:15 am (continuing all day).

Auction: Saturday, January 17 at 10:15 am and 2 pm.

Illustrated catalogue S4, S5 by mail. Order by sale no. 4523Y.

Exhibition: Friday, January 16.

Illustrated catalogue S6, S7 by mail. Order by sale no. 4524Y.

York Avenue Galleries

Victorian International

including Silver. Objects of Vertu, Glass, Pottery and Porcelain, Bronzes and Decorations, Furniture, Rugs and Tapestries.

Auction: Friday and Saturday. January 23 & 24 at 10:15 am and 2 pm each day.

Exhibition: Saturday, January 17 through Thursday, January 22.

Lecture: Sunday, January 18 at 2 pm in conjunction with this exhibition (open to the public).

Illustrated catalogue S10. S12 by mail. Order by sale no. 4526Y.

Shown: Pair of Vienna vases and covers. late 19th century. (lot 166)

Madison Avenue Galleries

American and European Paintings, Drawings, Prints, and Sculpture

Auction: Friday, January 23 at 10:15 am.

Exhibition: Saturday, January 17 through Thursday, January 22.

Illustrated catalogue S4, S5 by mail. Order by sale no. 4527M.

Shown: Charlotte E. Babb, *Thetis*, signed and dated 1878, watercolor on paper. 14 x 13 inches. (lot 228)

Vignelli and Associates, 1981–82

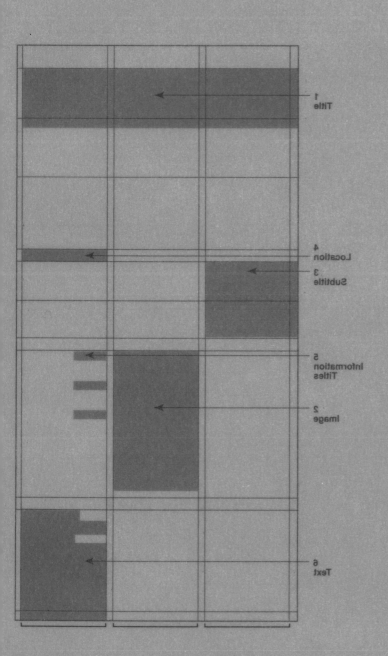

1
Title

4
Location

3
Subtitle

5
Information
Titles

2
Image

6
Text

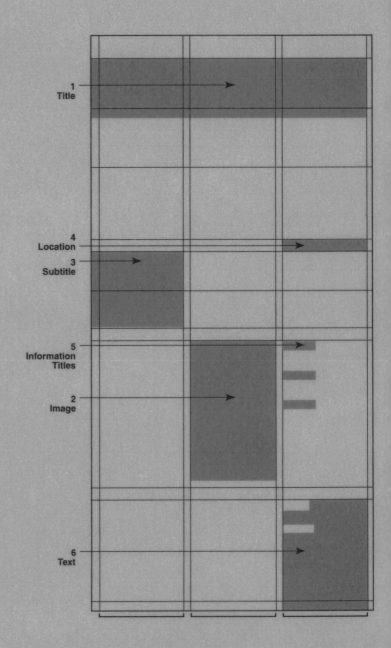

center

Table of Contents Spread for *The New Urban Landscape*

The contrast in texture of this spread by Drenttel Doyle Partners is immediately attractive. The title of the work is *The New Urban Landscape,* and the use of the entire spread for the table of contents speaks beautifully of the idea of the landscape.

The series of narrow columns of light text that move across the spread (shown on the overlay in black outline) create a rhythm

and repetition in the composition that give it a sense of order. The darker texture created by the bold text of the right page flows from top to bottom and is interrupted by long lines of text that span both pages. These long horizontal lines (shown on the overlay in light gray) serve both to communicate content and to unify the two pages as a single composition.

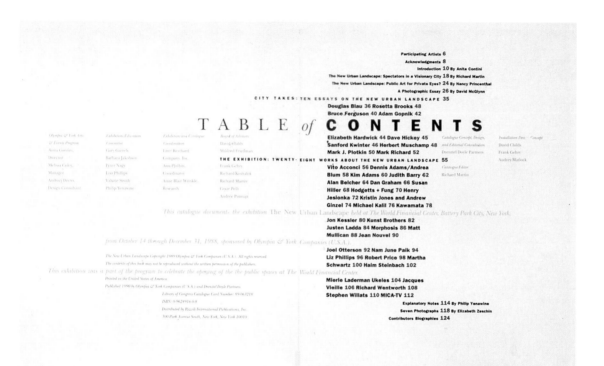

Drenttel Doyle Partners, 1988

The second in the series of exercises is the more complex, horizontal/vertical composition. The thumbnails for this set of compositions involve all of the visual theory mentioned previously and considerably more decisions regarding the choice or horizontal or vertical placement for each element.

The same visual principles of grouping, edge and axial alignment, and the law of thirds apply in this series. The resulting compositions are livelier due to the contrast in direction of the elements and variations in white space. Eye flow becomes an important consideration as text takes the place of the rectangle elements.

When substituting text for the rectangle elements, the question arises as to whether the text should read from top to bottom or bottom to top. The direction of reading depends on the composition and the way that the eye moves around it. Often the circle becomes a pivot point for the eye as it revolves around the composition. It should be noted that when surveying the spines of books in a library, there is an overwhelming number of books whose spine titles read top to bottom.

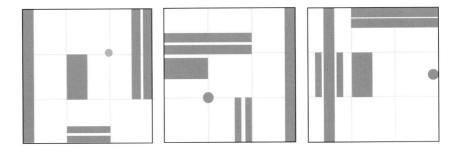

Because the first series of exercises were organized to guide the student through a thorough investigation of project variables, the organization of the second series occurs more naturally. The student has been sensitized to the nuances of composition, and it is not necessary to focus on specific compositional theory during the phases. The complexity of the project increases as each of the elements are used either horizontally or vertically.

Again, the longest element, the rectangle that spans all three visual fields, controls the composition. The major approaches still include top, bottom, and interior positions as well as the vertical positions of left, right, and interior. Compositional stability is most readily achieved with the longest rectangle placed near a perimeter edge: top, bottom, left, or right. When the longest rectangle is in this position it anchors the composition to the format and gives a sense of stability. Likewise, when the longest rectangle rests in the interior of the composition, either horizontal or vertical, the composition is less stable and more asymmetric.

Emphasis:
• Grouping
• Negative Space
• Perimeter Edge
• Axial Alignment
• The Law of Thirds
• Circle Placement
• Leading
• Reading Direction

Horizontal/Vertical Composition

Rotation of Composition
Each composition can be rotated to produce three additional compositions.

Series 1, 2, 3, 4
  Emphasis: • Grouping
            • Negative Space   All compositional aspects are
            • Perimeter Edge   emphasized with the addition
            • Axial Alignment   of reading direction. Reading
            • The Law of Thirds   direction is determined by the
            • Circle Placement   composition as a whole.
            • Leading
            • Reading Direction

Series 1, Long Rectangle in Top Position

Series 2, Long Rectangle in Bottom Position

Series 3, Long Rectangle in Left or Right Position

Series 4, Long Rectangle in Interior Position

Because the gray rectangle compositions are made with nonobjective elements, they can easily be rotated. This rotation exercise is interesting in determining where the visual weight of the longest line is the most comfortable and in seeing how the hierarchical order shifts with changes in position. Lines of text that are upside down after rotation are changed to read right side up.

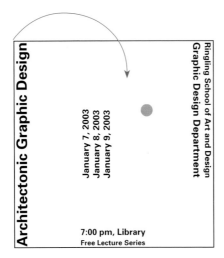

1. Original Composition

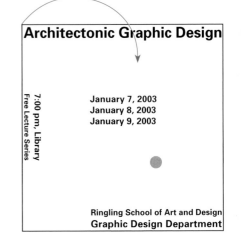

2. Second Composition
Rotated clockwise, 90º from original composition. Lines of text that are upside down are turned right side up.

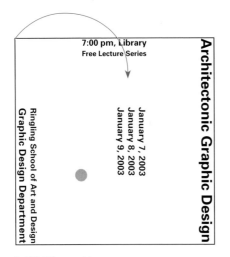

3. Third Composition
Rotated clockwise, 90º from second Icomposition. Lines of text that are upside down are turned right side up.

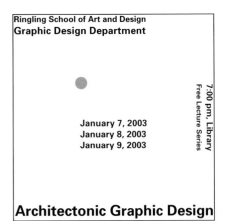

4. Fourth Composition
Rotated clockwise, 90º from third composition. Lines of text that are upside down are turned right side up.

Decisions regarding the direction of text, whether it will read top to bottom or bottom to top, should be made to be in concert with the other elements. In the top example, the vertical text reads bottom to top, which creates a comfortable clockwise reading order. In the lower example, the vertical text guides the eye off the page; there is a struggle to return to the top of the page and read the remainder of the message.

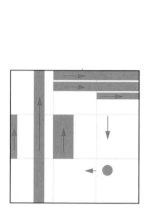

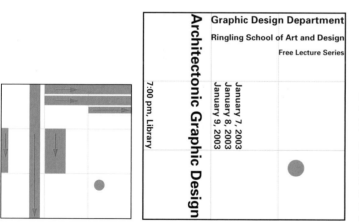

Clockwise Reading Direction
Vertical lines of text are oriented so that all elements read in a clockwise direction. This is visually comfortable for the reader.

Contrasting Reading Direction
Vertical lines of text are oriented to be in contrast with one another. This is visually uncomfortable for the reader as the eye struggles to move from one direction of text to the other. However, due to the brevity of the visual message, contrasting reading directions are not so uncomfortable that they should be disregarded.

With the long rectangle in the top position as a horizontal starting point, any or all of the other elements can be placed vertically. Since the two medium-sized rectangles, two units wide, are the next largest elements, attention is given to formulating their role in the composition by splitting their placement: one horizontal and one vertical, both horizontal, and both vertical.

The same goals of compositional cohesiveness that were present in the first series of compositions—grouping, negative space, perimeter edge, axial alignment, the law of thirds, circle placement, and leading—are also present in this series.

Medium Rectangles,
One Horizontal, One Vertical
Because the rectangles are arranged in contrasting directions, the negative spaces are more complex, and grouping and interior alignment become very important.

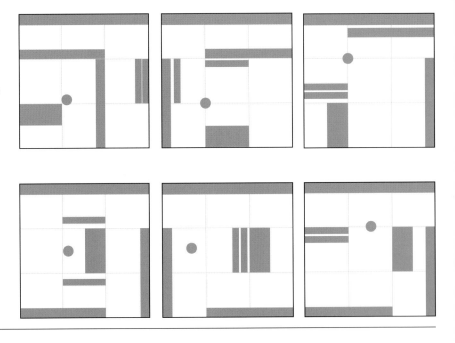

Medium Rectangles,
Both Horizontal
Because both rectangles are arranged in the same direction, the negative spaces are fewer and simpler.

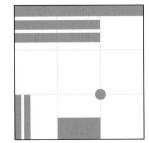
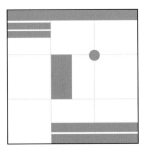
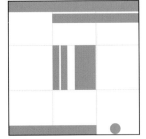

- **Grouping**
- **Negative Space**
- **Perimeter Edge**
- **Axial Alignment**
- **The Law of Thirds**
- **Circle Placement**
- **Leading**
- **Reading Direction**

Medium Rectangles,
Both Horizontal (continued)

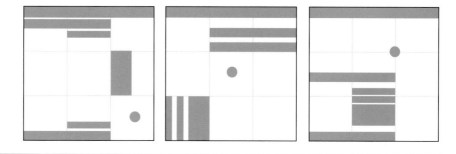

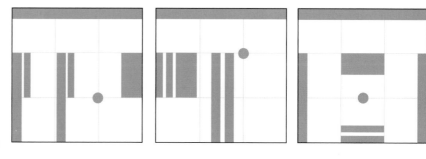

Medium Rectangles,
Both Vertical
A pleasing compositional arrangement is more difficult to achieve because the eye moves off of the bottom of the page where the vertical rectangles touch the bottom edge of the format. When this occurs the placement of the circle and the small one-unit rectangles can be arranged to lead the eye back into the composition.

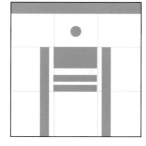

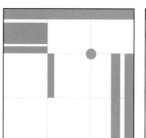

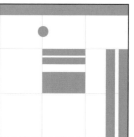

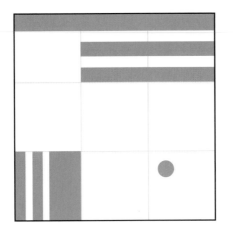

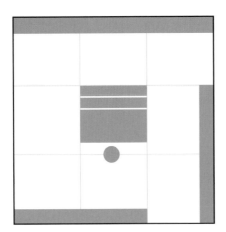

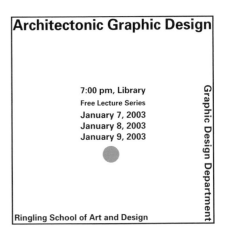

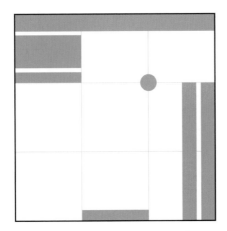

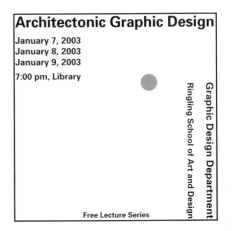

- **Grouping**
- **Negative Space**
- **Perimeter Edge**
- **Axial Alignment**
- **The Law of Thirds**
- **Circle Placement**
- **Leading**
- **Reading Direction**

Medium Rectangles,
One Horizontal, One Vertical
When contrasting directions
are used for similar elements,
grouping and interior alignment
become very important. Each
thumbnail example on the left
is followed by two variations
on that composition.

Medium Rectangles,
Both Horizontal
Because both rectangles are
arranged in the same direction,
the negative spaces are fewer
and simpler.

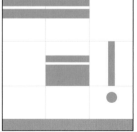
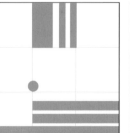

- **Grouping**
- **Negative Space**
- **Perimeter Edge**
- **Axial Alignment**
- **The Law of Thirds**
- **Circle Placement**
- **Leading**
- **Reading Direction**

Medium Rectangles,
Both Horizontal (continued)

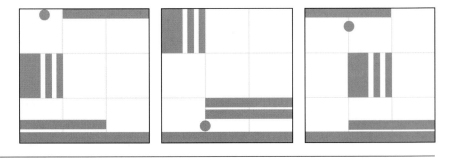

Medium Rectangles,
Both Vertical
A pleasing composition is
more difficult to achieve in this
arrangement, and, frequently,
the small one-unit rectangles
must be placed in the same
direction, all vertical or all
horizontal, for unity.

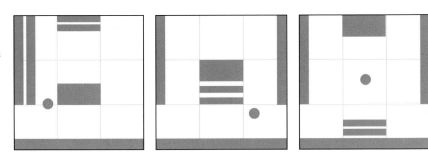

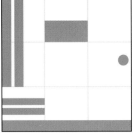
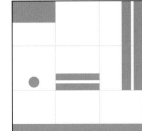
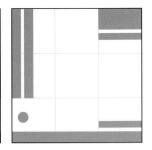

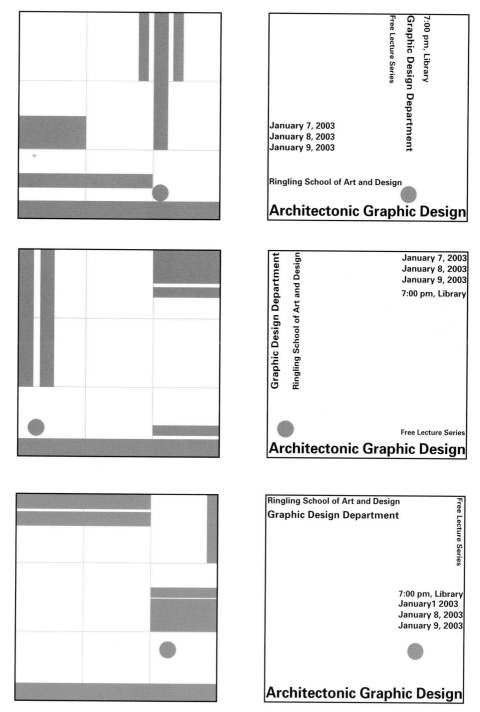

Poster 1 (top right):

7:00 pm, Library
Graphic Design Department
Free Lecture Series

January 7, 2003
January 8, 2003
January 9, 2003

Ringling School of Art and Design

Architectonic Graphic Design

Poster 2 (middle right):

Graphic Design Department
Ringling School of Art and Design

January 7, 2003
January 8, 2003
January 9, 2003

7:00 pm, Library

Free Lecture Series

Architectonic Graphic Design

Poster 3 (bottom right):

Ringling School of Art and Design
Graphic Design Department

Free Lecture Series

7:00 pm, Library
January1 2003
January 8, 2003
January 9, 2003

Architectonic Graphic Design

- **Grouping**
- **Negative Space**
- **Perimeter Edge**
- **Axial Alignment**
- **The Law of Thirds**
- **Circle Placement**
- **Leading**
- **Reading Direction**

Medium Rectangles,
Both Horizontal
Because both rectangles are
arranged in the same direction,
the negative spaces are fewer,
simpler, and compositional
unity is readily achieved.

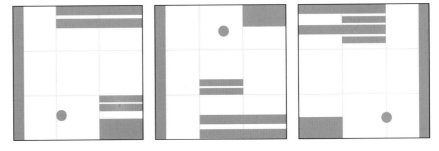

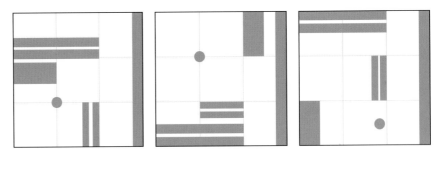

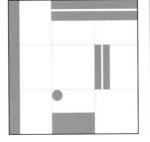

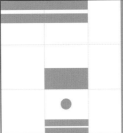

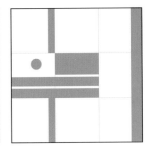

- **Grouping**
- **Negative Space**
- **Perimeter Edge**
- **Axial Alignment**
- **The Law of Thirds**
- **Circle Placement**
- **Leading**
- **Reading Direction**

Medium Rectangles,
Both Horizontal (continued)

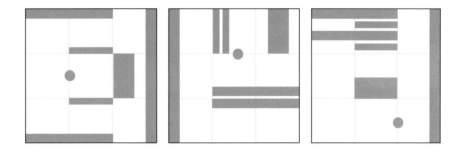

Medium Rectangles,
Both Vertical
Because both rectangles are
arranged in the same direction,
the negative spaces are fewer
and simpler.

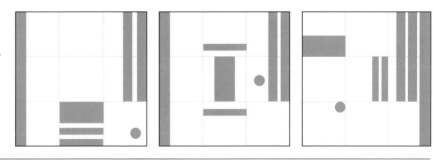

Medium Rectangles,
One Horizontal, One Vertical
The simplest composition is
achieved with the medium
rectangles arranged against
the right and bottom edges.
When the medium rectangles
occupy space in the interior of
the composition, the result is
more complex.

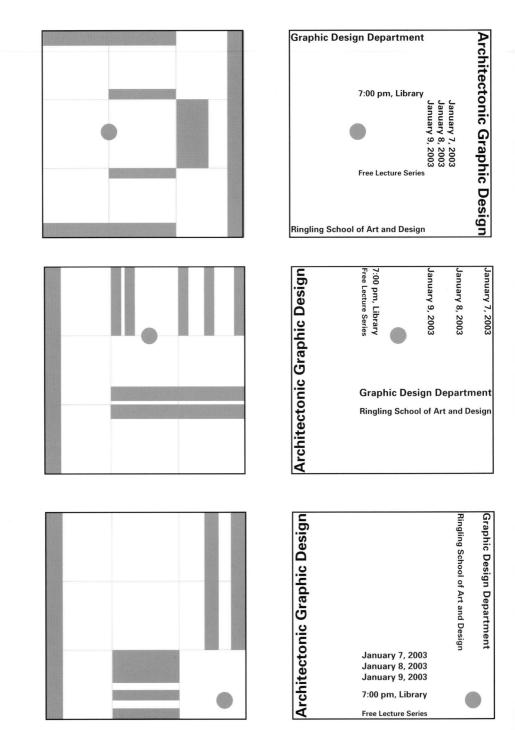

The least comfortable position for the longest rectangle is in the exact center of the format. This position divides the space equally and is less interesting than the asymmetric arrangements. Shifting this interior position creates a more interesting proportion.

- **Grouping**
- **Negative Space**
- **Perimeter Edge**
- **Axial Alignment**
- **The Law of Thirds**
- **Circle Placement**
- **Leading**
- **Reading Direction**

Medium Rectangles,
Both Horizontal
Because both rectangles are arranged in the same direction, the negative spaces are fewer, simpler, and compositional unity is readily achieved.

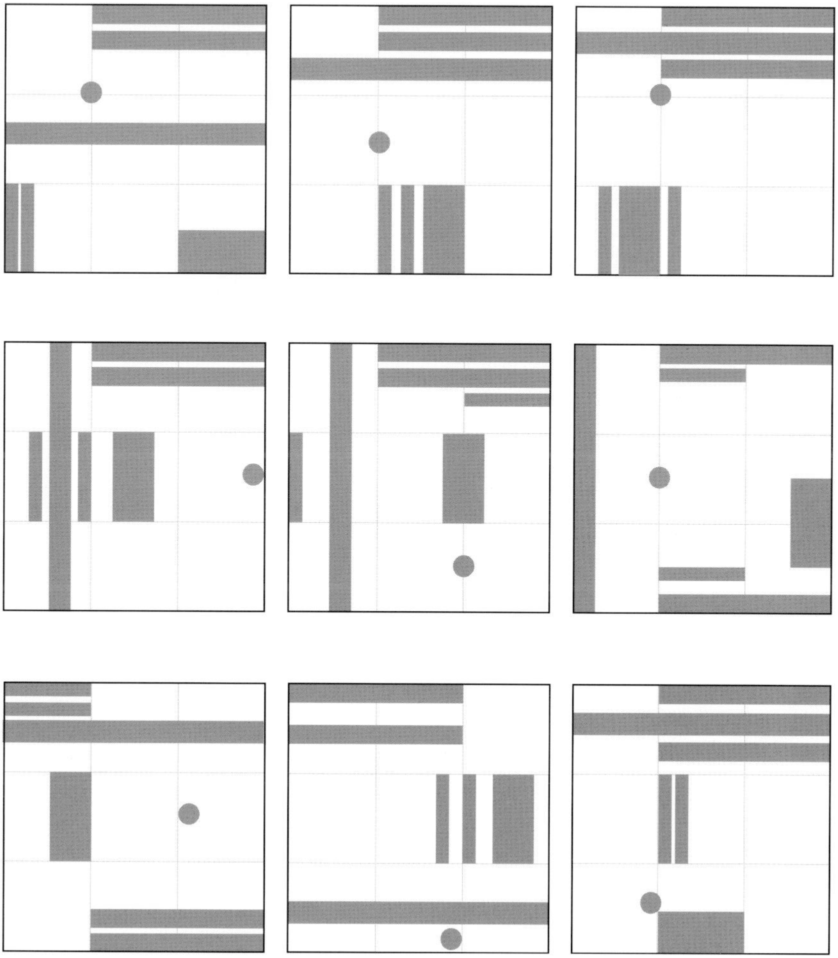

- **Grouping**
- **Negative Space**
- **Perimeter Edge**
- **Axial Alignment**
- **The Law of Thirds**
- **Circle Placement**
- **Leading**
- **Reading Direction**

Medium Rectangles,
Both Horizontal (continued)

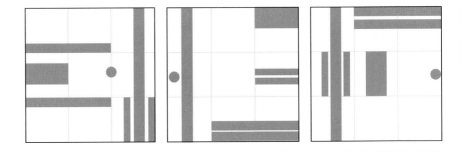

Medium Rectangles,
Both Vertical
Because both rectangles are
arranged in the same direction,
the negative spaces are fewer
and simpler.

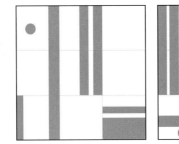

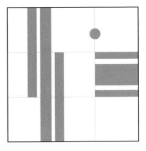

Medium Rectangles,
One Horizontal, One Vertical
The simplest composition is
achieved with the medium
rectangles arranged against
the edges. When the medium
rectangles occupy space in
the interior of the composition,
the result is more complex.

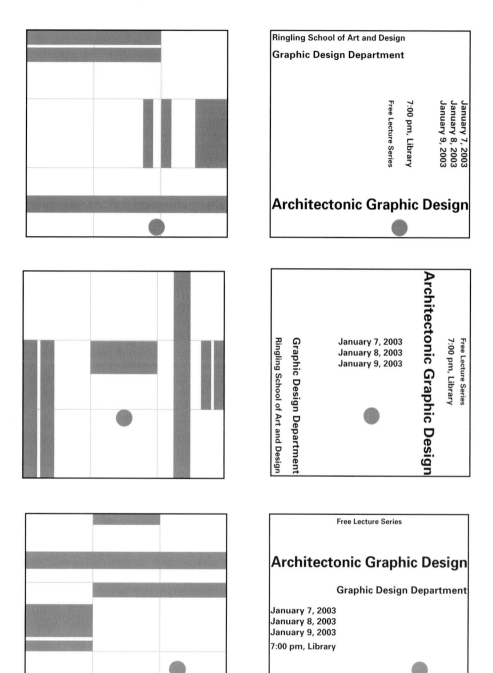

Ringling School of Art and Design

Graphic Design Department

January 7, 2003
January 8, 2003
January 9, 2003

7:00 pm, Library

Free Lecture Series

Architectonic Graphic Design

Architectonic Graphic Design

Free Lecture Series
7:00 pm, Library

January 7, 2003
January 8, 2003
January 9, 2003

Graphic Design Department

Ringling School of Art and Design

Free Lecture Series

Architectonic Graphic Design

Graphic Design Department

January 7, 2003
January 8, 2003
January 9, 2003

7:00 pm, Library

Ringling School of Art and Design

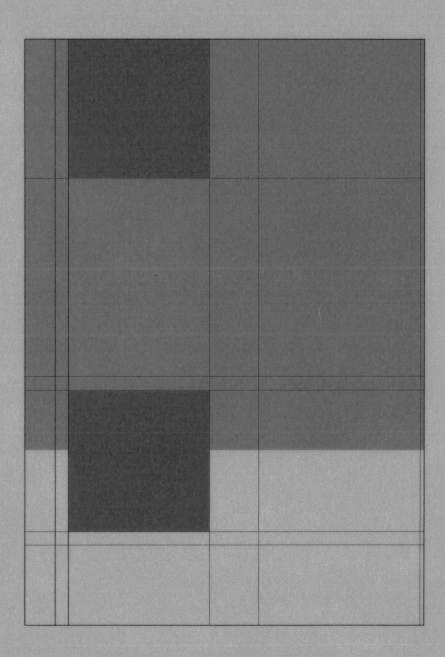

Both the color and design are striking in Richard P. Lohse's *Zürcher Künstler im Helmhaus* poster. The colors are a play on the complimentary contrast of red and green. Instead of a primary green, a pastel green is activated with a saturated bright red. The vertical text rests in a background window created with a white rectangle and is repeated horizontally in the foreground. The heavy red rule acts as a frame for the foreground text and marries the two text blocks together.

Richard P. Lohse, 1950

These are pages from a catalog of seasonal products for outdoor-industry professionals and athletes. The typography appears on the vertical in a band that spans the spread. The band is punctuated by solid vertical rules that change color and reverse out the product name. The descriptive text follows the vertical rule, with size and pricing information in bold. The rules and text have the option to flow across the gutter from the left page onto the right page. The images float in between bands of text as vignettes.

Design Firm
Nike Inc., Beaverton, Oregon

Creative Director
Michael Verdine

Designer
Angelo Colletti, 2002

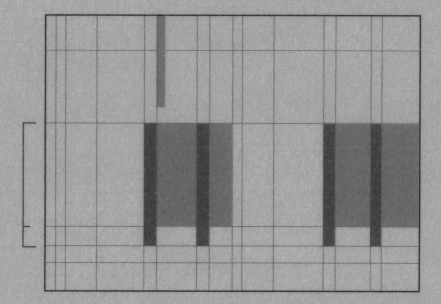

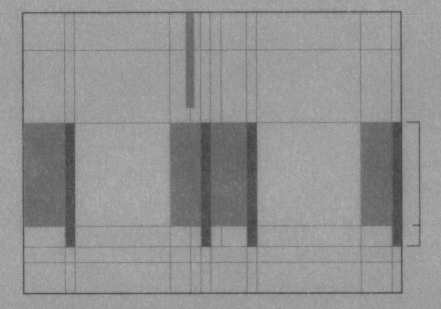

Siegfried Odermatt and Rosmarie Tissi, Odermatt & Tissi, use classical structures of typographic organization in fresh and innovative ways. The color is bright and eye catching and the compositions always cohesive. The poster for the 150th Anniversary of Zurich University is only two colors, blue and black, printed on white paper but seems rich and more lively—irregular shapes that are tailored around the typography pop out of the page. The extreme thicks and thins of the vertical Bodoni type contrast the blunt shapes. The vertical type creates the grid lines that determine the flush-right alignment of the white shapes and flush-left alignment of the horizontal black text. The placement of the umlauts next to the A and inside the U is a delightful detail.

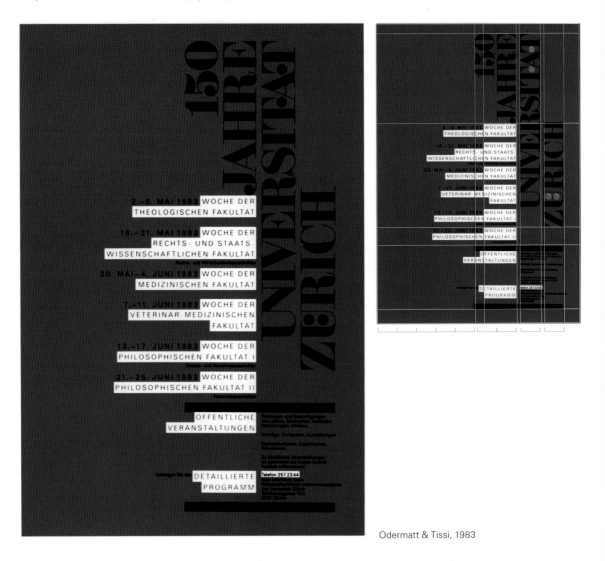

Odermatt & Tissi, 1983

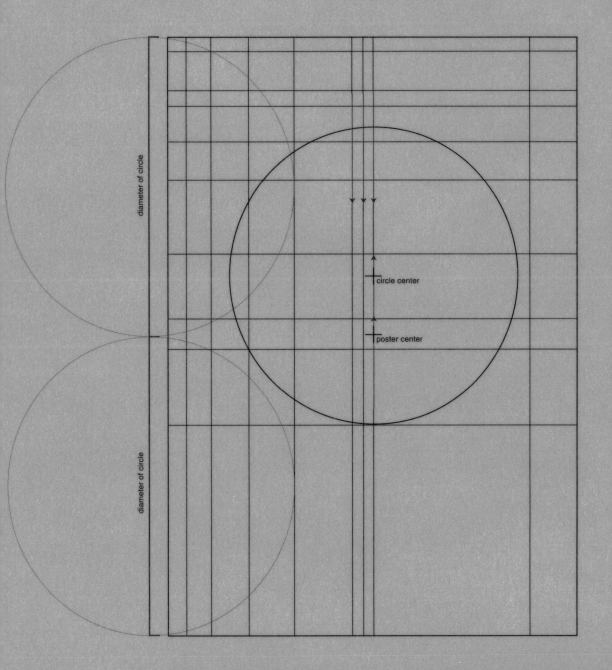

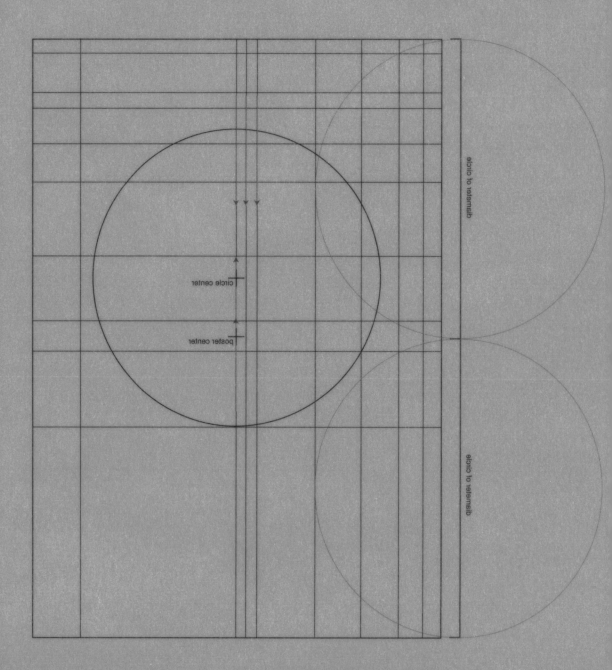

diameter of circle

circle center

poster center

diameter of circle

The *Best of Swiss Posters of the Year 1992*, also by Odermatt & Tissi, has some delightful and subtle nuances. The Swiss cross in white aligns with the arc at top and bottom as well as the left edge of the text at the top of the poster. The diameter of the circle is one-half the height of the poster. The thin repetitive rules at the top and the heavier white rules at the left create rhythms as the eye moves down the page and returns to the top by the arc. Compositional unity is achieved as the eye moves horizontally, vertically, and in a circle with the Swiss cross as a pivot point. The function of the Swiss cross is similar to the circle in the previous compositional exercises.

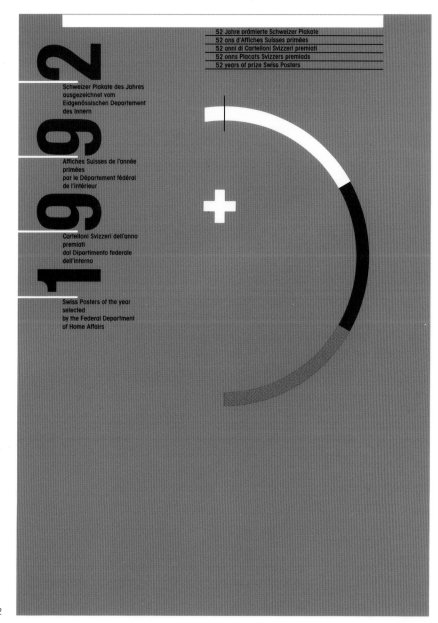

Odermatt & Tissi, 1992

Festival d'été (Summer Festival), Program Spread

This spread, although complex in direction, nonobjective elements, and text, reads quite clearly. The pages are separate, yet are part of a whole. The compositional unity is due to the use of a similar grid on both pages and the alignment of elements from page to page. The four columns of text have a similar line length and a common top horizon. The rules align on both pages and the vertical text is set inside a series of rhythmical rules that connotate a musical staff.

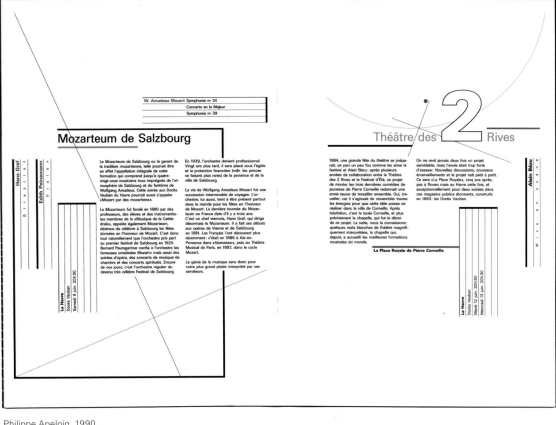

Philippe Apeloig, 1990

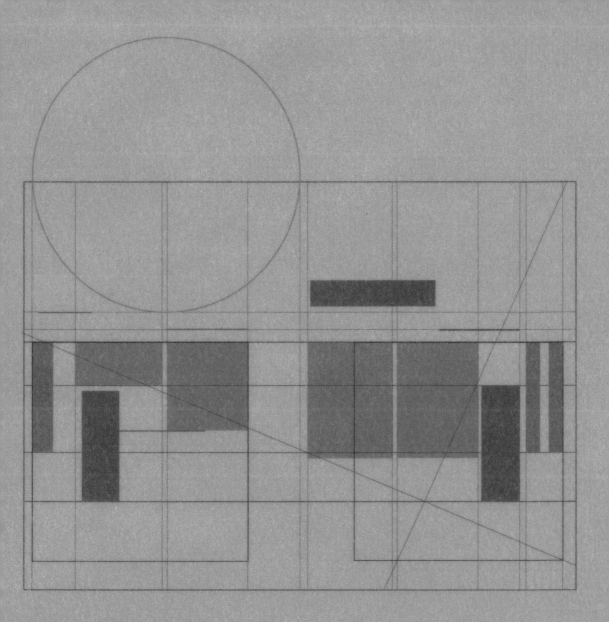

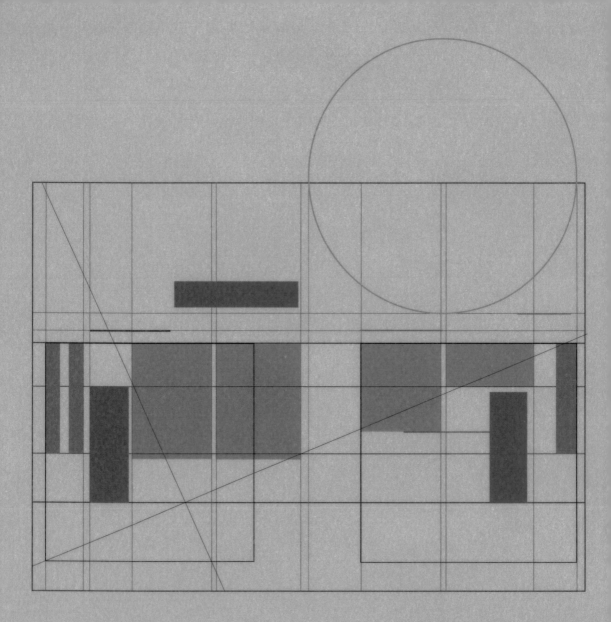

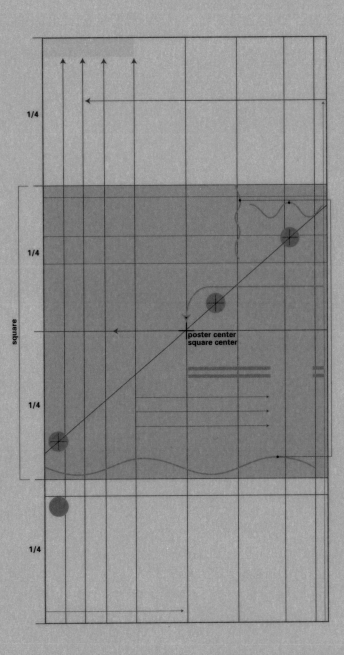

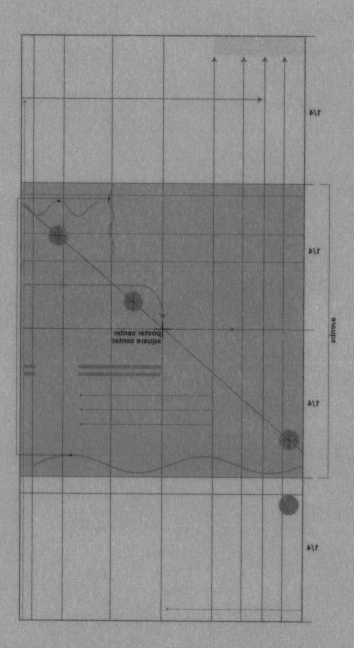

poster center
square center

1/4

1/4

square

1/4

1/4

This poster is by Willi Kunz for Columbia University's Graduate School of Architecture and Planning. The poster announces a new graduate-degree program in historic preservation. The square photograph of an architectural detail occupies the foreground and is in contrast to the rectangular format. The nonobjective elements, the circles and wavy lines, echo the details found in the photo.

The aesthetic is architectonic and appropriate for a school of architecture. The vertical lines of type act as columns in contrast to the square photograph and the green graphic field. These lines of text align with the horizontal shadow of the photograph and with the three vertical hairlines in the top black rule. There is a purposefulness to each compositional element and a direct relationship to other elements within the poster.

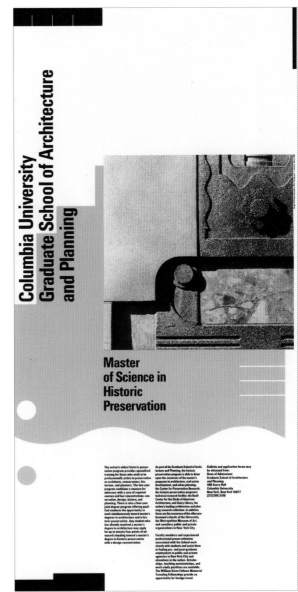

Willi Kunz, 2000

Diagonal Composition

The most dynamic and the most complex compositional direction is the diagonal. The three-column by three-row grid structure does not easily accommodate the diagonal direction because of the scale of the elements. Reducing the scale of the elements by 15 percent allows the elements to fit within the format and have more compositional flexibility.

The reduced 3 X 3 diagonal grid is placed in the format but, as the designer begins to compose, the alignment of edges and corners takes precedence over a formal fixed structure. While the structure is still used for organization and alignment, it is less important than in the previous compositions.

There is an opportunity in this composition to place elements at 45° angles or at 30°/60° angles. In addition, the rotation of elements can be in a clockwise direction or a counter-clockwise direction, and, therefore, the decision-making process is more complex.

The focus is on creating an alignment for each element that has a direct relationship with another element. The most visually cohesive compositions have multiple alignments of elements and, as with the previous compositions, no element is without a partner. The exception to this is the use of an anomaly or an element whose position and/or rotation is in direct contrast to the other elements—diversity within unity.

Rotating 45°
When the composition elements are reduced in scale by 15 percent (far right) and the positions are readjusted, they fit more comfortably in the format.

45° Diagonal
Elements may be placed at a
45° diagonal rotated clockwise
or counter clockwise.

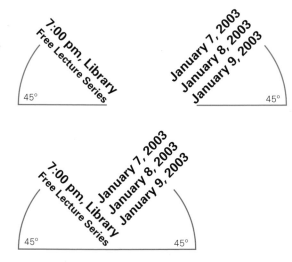

30°/60° Diagonal
Elements may be placed at a
30° diagonal or 60° diagonal.

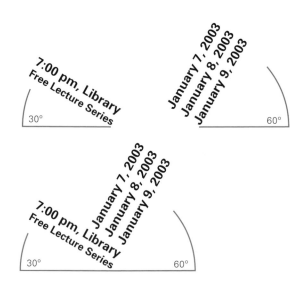

The diagonal compositions are the most complex of the series. Elements can be composed in a single direction or contrasting directions, and the negative spaces that are created are triangles. Placement of the 3 X 3 grid structure in the square format is a variable, and the opportunity exists to create tensions with the perimeter of the format.

Compositions with elements strictly in one direction, such as the 45° diagonal and the 30° diagonal below, have a sense of harmony because all of the elements read in a single direction. Compositions with elements that have an opposing diagonal have heightened visual interest because of the contrast in direction, such as the 45°/45° diagonal and the 30°/ 60° diagonal.

Emphasis:
• Grouping
• Negative Space
• Perimeter Edge
• Axial Alignment
• The Law of Thirds
• Circle Placement
• Leading
• Reading Direction
• Edge Tension

Diagonal Composition

Grid Placement
Each composition can be placed near a format edge to create tension.

Series 1, 2, 3, 4
       Emphasis: • Grouping
                   • Negative Space
                   • Perimeter Edge
                   • Axial Alignment
                   • The Law of Thirds
                   • Circle Placement
                   • Leading
                   • Reading Direction
                   • Edge Tension

All compositional aspects are emphasized with the addition of edge tension. Edge tensions may be created by placing elements near the edges.

Series 1, Single Direction
45°

Series 2, Contrasting Directions
45°/45°

Series 3, Single Direction
30° or 60°

Series 4, Contrasting Directions
30°/60°

Since the grid and elements are reduced to 85 percent and placed on an angle, there are options as to where the grid and elements are placed inside the square format. Tensions may be created by placing elements near the edges and by the positioning of the circle.

Because of the dynamic qualities of the diagonal, when placed close to an edge, there is movement in the composition. The circle can enhance this dynamic quality by becoming either a stopping or starting point.

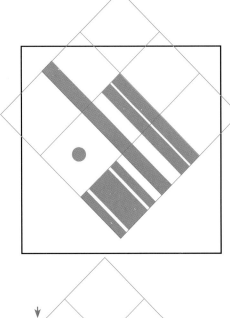

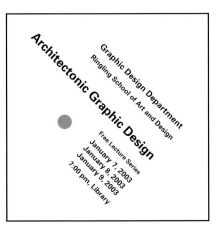

No Tension
Composition is placed in a square format and is floating, with white space at all four edges.

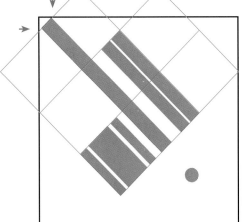

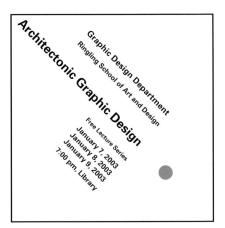

Tension at Upper Left Corner

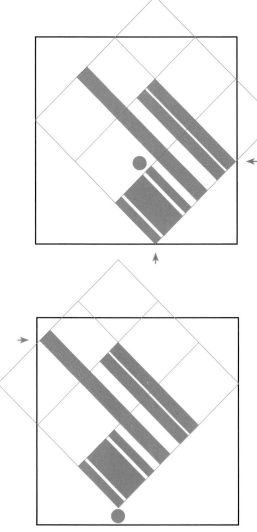

Tension at Right and Bottom Edge

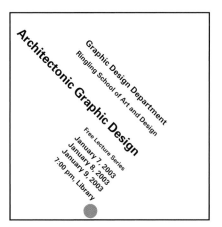

Tension with Circle at Bottom Edge

The rectangle elements of a 45° composition point toward the corners of the format, and the resulting negative spaces are primarily symmetrical 45°–90°–45° triangles (example below). These triangles are anchored to the format because their sides rest on the perimeter edges. The resulting compositions are harmonious due to the repetition of the triangle and the anchoring to the format.

When the rectangles are arranged on a 45° diagonal, the first decision is whether the rectangles will be rotated in a clock-

wise or counter-clockwise direction. There is no compositional advantage to either choice and both directions yield equally valid results. However, different reading directions occur when lines of text are substituted for the gray rectangles. Lines that are rotated 45° clockwise read from upper left to lower right (opposite page top row). Lines that are rotated 45° counter clockwise read from lower left to upper right (opposite page center row). Because most reading begins in the upper left corner of the page, it is slightly easier to read compositions that are rotated clockwise.

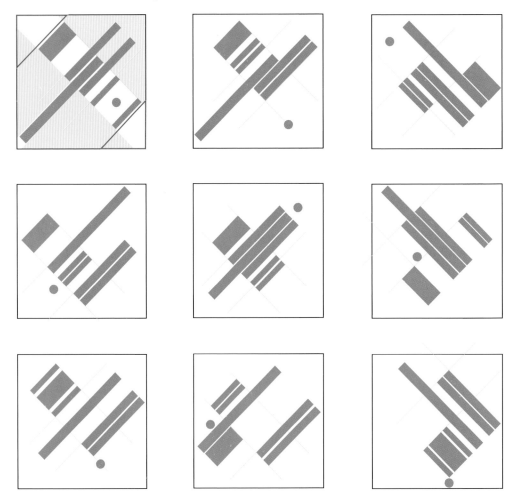

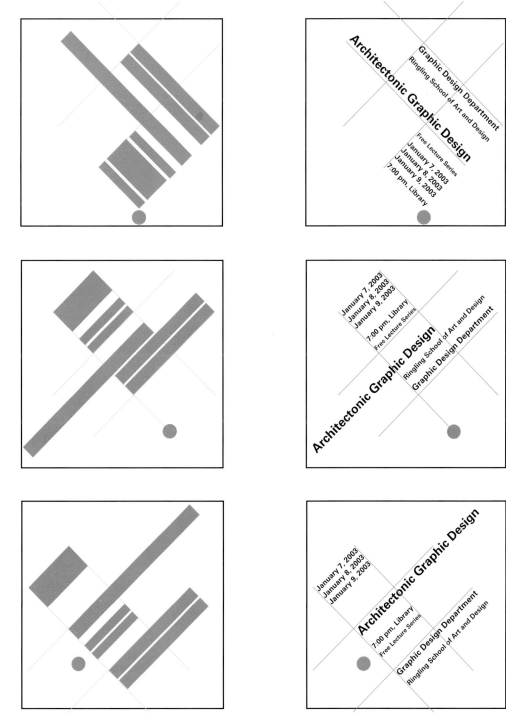

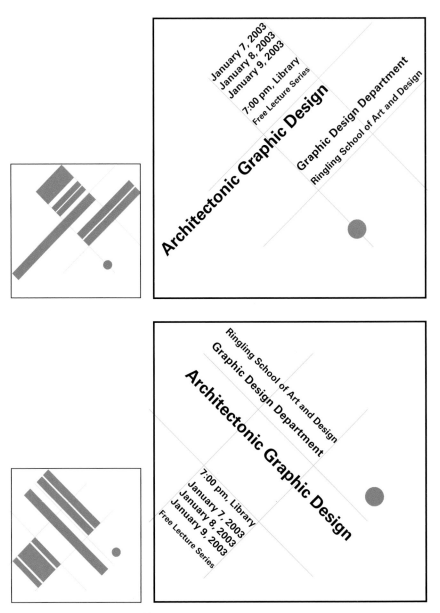

January 7, 2003
January 8, 2003
January 9, 2003

7:00 pm, Library
Free Lecture Series

Architectonic Graphic Design

Graphic Design Department
Ringling School of Art and Design

Ringling School of Art and Design
Graphic Design Department

Architectonic Graphic Design

7:00 pm, Library
January 7, 2003
January 8, 2003
January 9, 2003
Free Lecture Series

Contrasting direction compositions combine rectangles that are rotated clockwise and counter clockwise. The compositions are more complex, interesting, and livelier because the negative spaces are divided by elements moving in two directions. Negative spaces consist of implied triangles and rectangles that frequently intersect.

- **Grouping**
- **Negative Space**
- **Perimeter Edge**
- **Axial Alignment**
- **The Law of Thirds**
- **Circle Placement**
- **Leading**
- **Reading Direction**
- **Edge Tension**

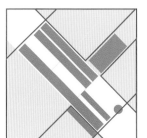

79

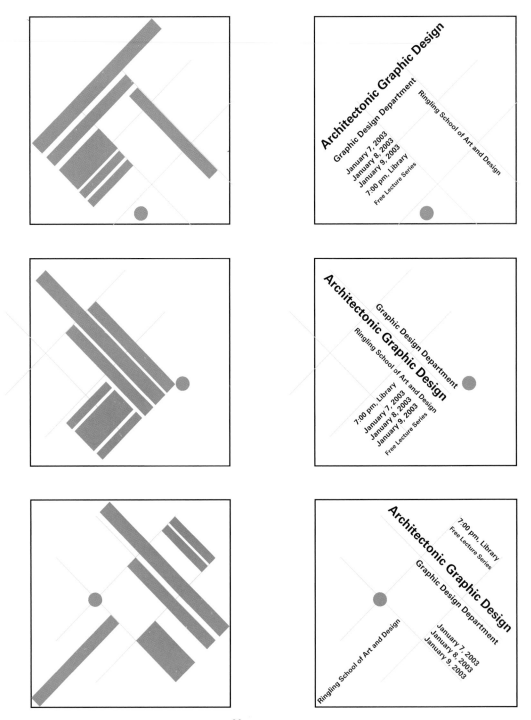

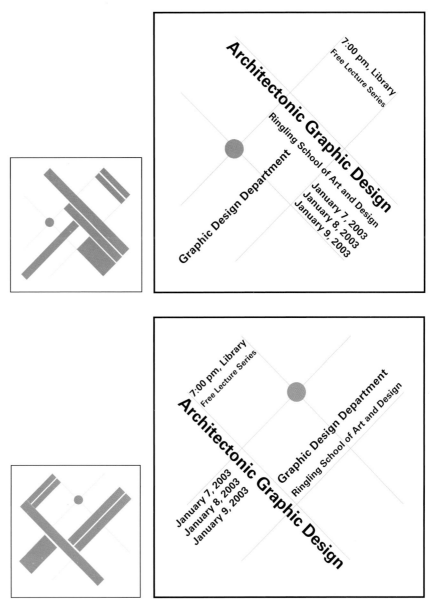

Instead of the symmetrical triangles of negative space found in the 45° compositions, the triangles created in the 30° and 60° compositions are 30°–60°–90° right triangles. These right triangles are more dynamic because the vertex angle is narrower and they are asymmetric.

- **Grouping**
- **Negative Space**
- **Perimeter Edge**
- **Axial Alignment**
- **The Law of Thirds**
- **Circle Placement**
- **Leading**
- **Reading Direction**
- **Edge Tension**

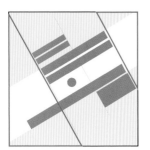

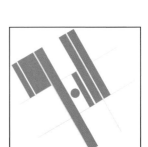

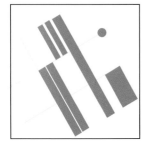

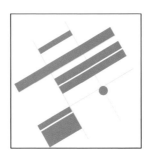

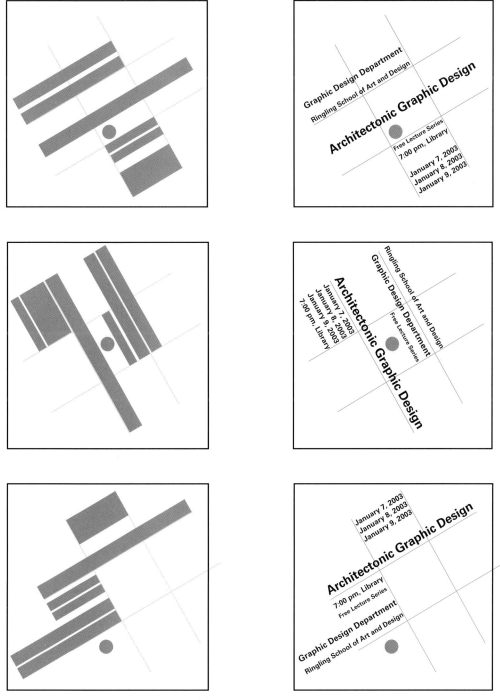

Ringling School of Art and Design

7:00 pm, Library

Graphic Design Department

Free Lecture Series

Architectonic Graphic Design

January 7, 2003

January 8, 2003

January 9, 2003

Architectonic Graphic Design

7:00 pm, Library

Free Lecture Series

January 7, 2003
January 8, 2003
January 9, 2003

Graphic Design Department

Ringling School of Art and Design

Contrasting direction compositions combine rectangles that are rotated 30° or 60° clockwise and counter clockwise. Similar to the 45° compositions, the results are often more complex, interesting, and livelier because the negative spaces are divided by elements moving in two directions at two different angles. Negative spaces consist of implied triangles and rectangles that frequently intersect or overlap.

- **Grouping**
- **Negative Space**
- **Perimeter Edge**
- **Axial Alignment**
- **The Law of Thirds**
- **Circle Placement**
- **Leading**
- **Reading Direction**
- **Edge Tension**

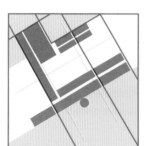
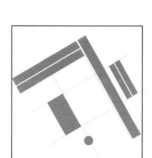

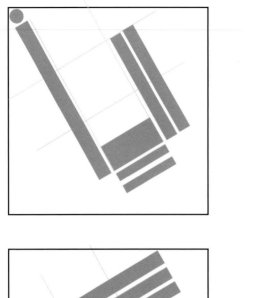

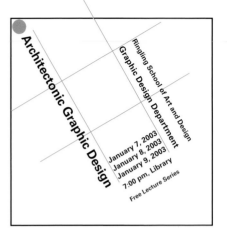

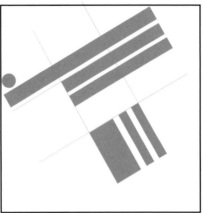

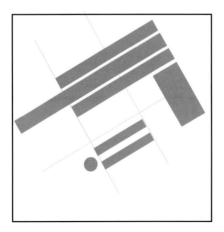

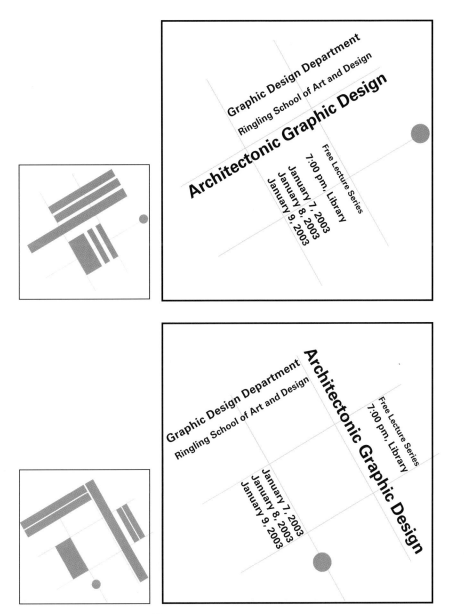

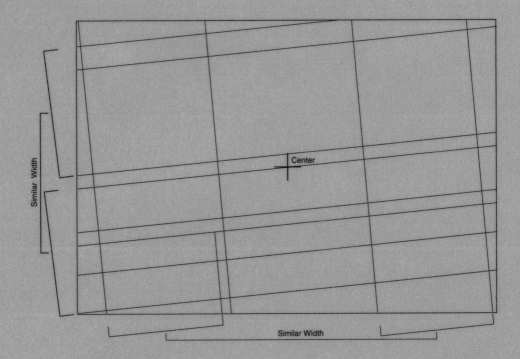

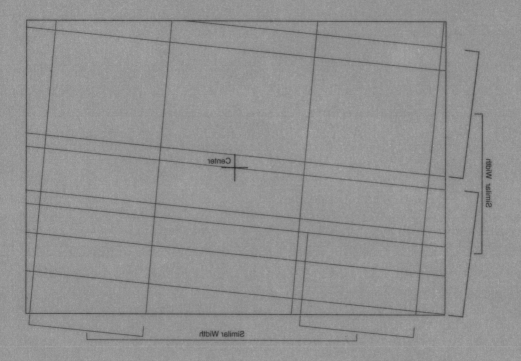

Kandinsky Poster

Herbert Bayer was a student of Wassily Kandinsky at the Bauhaus and produced this poster for an exhibition of Kandinsky's paintings on his sixtieth birthday.

Since the poster was almost certainly produced with letterpress, it must have been composed horizontally. Through digital image manipulation, the poster was rotated to the horizontal and appears below the original. While the horizontal version is still appealing, the dynamic character of the original diagonal poster is heightened with the comparison.

The use of primary color, sans serif typography, and rectangular red rules as devices of organization and emphasis are in keeping with constructivist principles. The use of the diagonal makes this poster unique and outstanding. Since the poster was produced by letterpress with a photo engraving, the work was probably composed in the horizontal/vertical letterpress lock-up system and rotated 7.5° when printed.

Herbert Bayer, 1926

Horizontal Version
The original Kandinsky poster (above) has been digitally manipulated to a horizontal format for comparison purposes.

Henryk Berlewi was a Polish designer who was profoundly influenced by a lecture series given by El Lissitzky in Warsaw in 1922. He moved to Berlin and began working on a series of typographic experiments that employed geometry, and primary colors, and were composed with "mechanical constructivism." *Reklama Mechano* is a page from a booklet of works from Berlewi's advertising agency of the same name. The pages were two-dimensional works that meshed geometric, mathematical compositions with informational text.

H. N. Werkman was also fascinated by printing and typography because "printing offers more possibilities than painting. It enables me to express myself more freely, and also more directly." This resulted in fine art experiments more akin to painting than to the functional communication that was influential at that time and today.

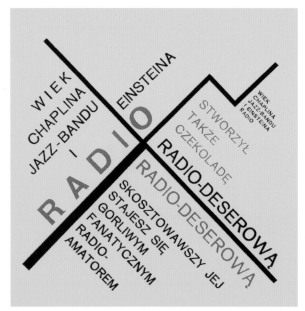

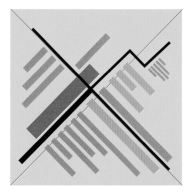

Abstracted Version
The original version is reduced to a series of rectangles on the yellow ground.

Henryk Berlewi, 1924

H. N. Werkman, 1924

The stark simplicity of Karl Gerstner's *National-Zeitung* poster is an excellent example of the Swiss international style. This style, begun in the 1950s, is similar to earlier Bauhaus works in that it focused on asymmetry, functional sans serif typography, a high level of visual organization, and an absence of decorative imagery.

Gerstner's poster for the newspaper, *National-Zeitung*, clearly and simply states the range of news from local, national, and international sources. The diagonal grid is sharpened by turning the word "Zeitung" ninety degrees and allowing the N to also function as a Z. Repetition and alignment of the letter forms in the words create a pattern. The alignment of the letter "l" at the end of the four words forms a long rule that enhances the diagonal. The first l in the word "lokal" and the letter "i" in the interior of the other three words also align and enhance the crisp organization. Finally, the dot on the first i of "international" is near the left edge of the poster and creates visual tension.

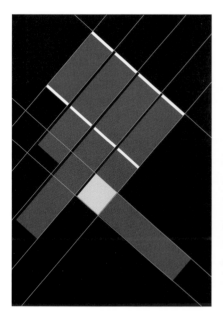

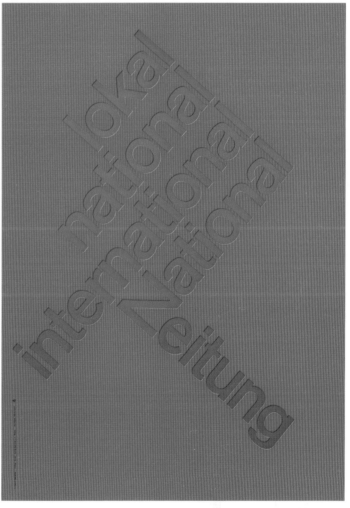

Karl Gerstner, 1960

Title Page Studies for the Freiburg Municipal Theatre

These variations in diagonal grid design by Emil Ruder appear in his book *Typography*. Ruder taught typography at the Allegemeine Gewerbeschule in Basel, Switzerland, and advocated functional readability and systematic typography structures in his courses. The examples show some of the variations possible within a harmonious diagonal grid.

Similar to the exercises in this book, the study is limited to communicating the same message with one type face, one weight, and one size of type. The variations occur in composition and all compositions are organized on the same 20° diagonal. Because of the rectangular format, there is flexibility in the length of the lines in the compositions. The groups of text can be near any edge and tensions between the text and edges are readily created. The lines are broken into one, two, or three words, and the reading direction is carefully controlled.

Emil Ruder, 1977

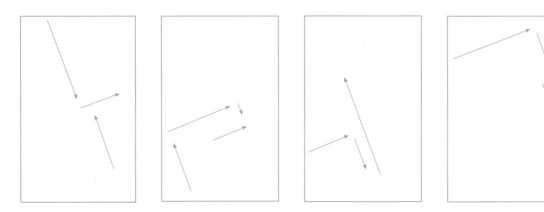

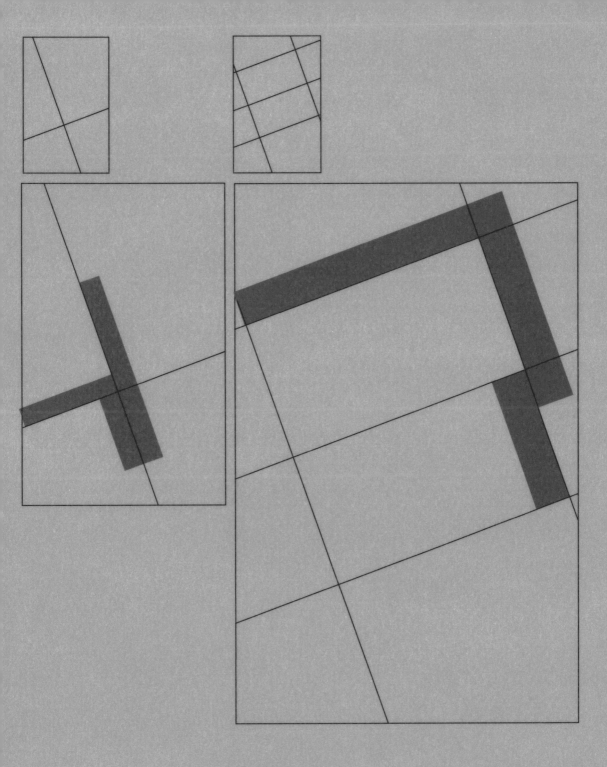

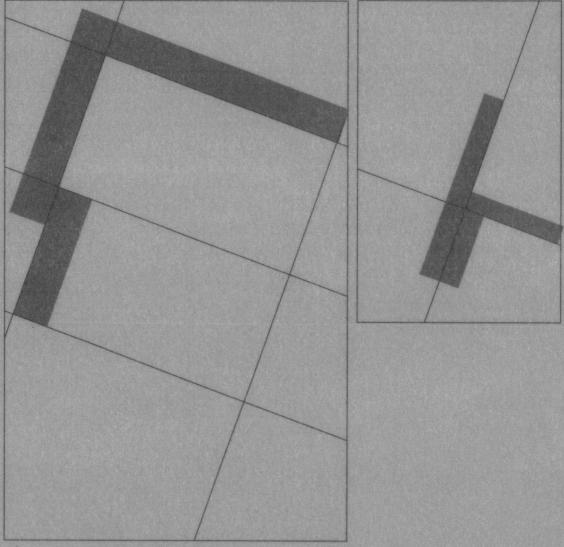

städtische bühnen

freiburg im breisgau

städtische bühnen
freiburg im breisgau
bühnen

städtische bühnen
freiburg im breisgau

Willi Kunz was born and educated in Switzerland and, since 1970, has made the United States his home. In his book *Typography: Macro + Micro Aesthetics*, he chronicles his own work and approach to typographic composition as well as his approach to teaching typography. Kunz writes, "Typographic design is realized on two aesthetic scales: macro (explicit and obvious) and micro (subtle, sophisticated, perhaps only subconsciously perceptible)."

Although complex, this poster communicates very clearly. The first visual analysis of this poster does not seem to bring much coherence into the design structure because of the variation in forms, angles, and color. However, reducing the poster to three levels, as Kunz does with another poster in *Typography*, begins to reveal insight into the structure.

The first layer holds a texture of multiple fine rules that are shaped at the top and bottom with a pattern of obtuse triangles down the middle. This layer serves as the compositional glue that connects the other layers. Each layer of the poster is a cohesive composition on its own and, when combined, the layers support and unify each other.

The second layer consists of the brightest solid orange elements, the rectangles and a circle. The horizontal rectangles flow down the page with changes in angles and an increase in length. The two long, narrow orange rectangles at each edge stabilize the composition. The two parallel vertical rectangles are echoed in a smaller version near the bottom.

The third layer consists of the typographic information. Facts are grouped according to content and, even with the changes in the angle, are easy to read. Each group has a distinct texture, with the more important information in bold. The four groups of text containing the lecturer's name, date of presentation, and biographical information are arranged in the same manner. This system allows the information to be easily read and understood. It is this diversity within unity that makes the composition so harmonious.

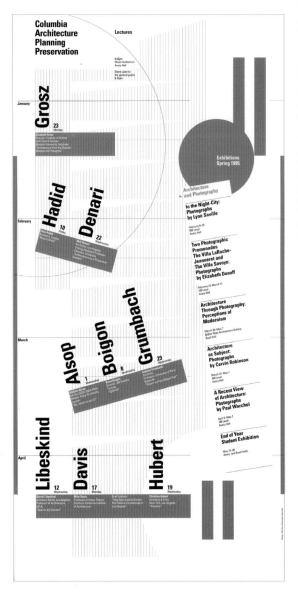

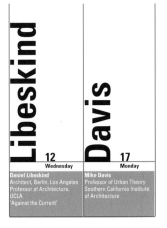

Group Systemization
Each group of names is organized with a common system of size, weight, and color.

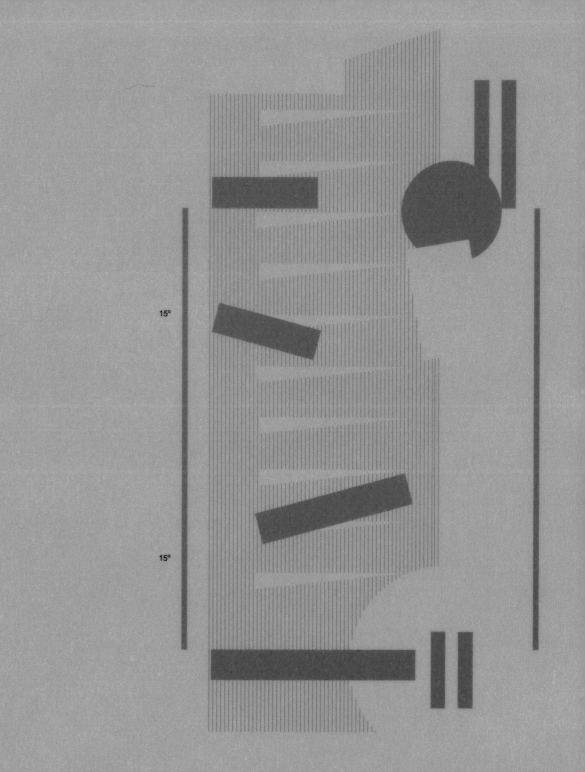

15°

15°

10°

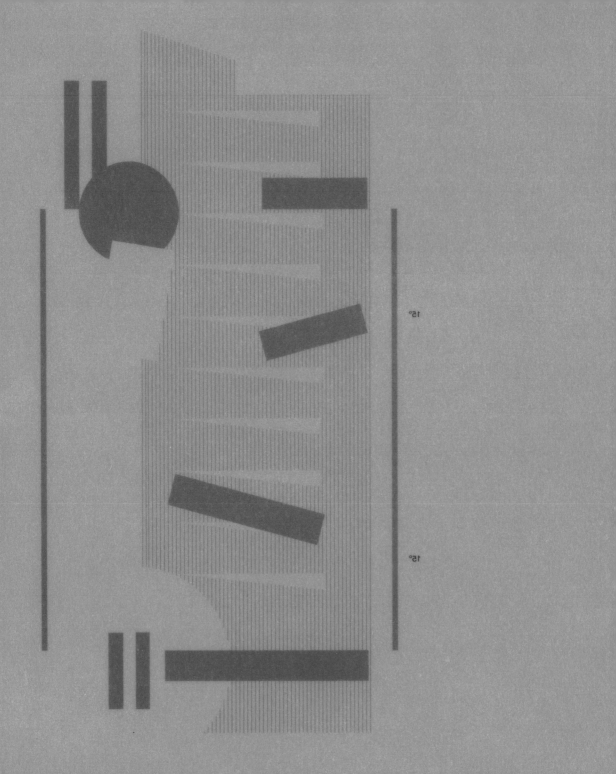

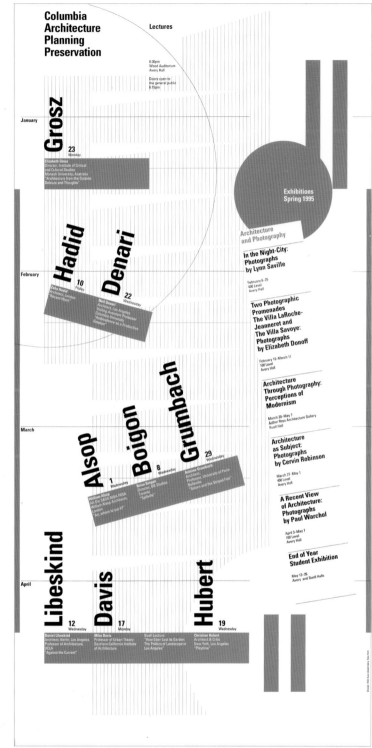

Willi Kunz, 1995

All visual messages have a hierarchal order to the information presented, that is, an order of reading the information according to importance. It is essential for the designer to determine a logical hierarchal order for all elements within a message before beginning design. Knowledge and understanding of the content of the message is essential for this process. Once the content has been organized, the designer can rationally make visual decisions that support that order.

In this series of projects, students select a historic date and develop a title and paragraph of descriptive copy. Each selection must have a title, day, year, and description paragraph. Using only one type face, size, weight, slope, and color, the student explores the variability of text element position in relationship to hierarchy by consciously ordering the content of the message.

Visual Message Content

Title   Identification of the AIDS Virus

Day   April 23

Year   1984

Text   Identification of a virus thought to cause Acquired Immunodeficiency Syndrome (AIDS) was announced by federal researchers on April 23, 1984. The disease destroys the body's natural immune system and is considered to be ultimately fatal. By the date of discovery, AIDS was estimated to have killed 4,000 Americans.

Kathy Azada, 1996

As the variables of the history project are investigated, the essential elements of managing text blocks are discovered. Initially, an auto lead at 20 percent of the type size, the default leading mode on the computer, is the only variation in leading employed. Through repetition and experimentation, the visual variety of texture and the subsequent changes in meaning and readability through texture change is apparent.

Sans serif faces such as Helvetica and Univers 65, which is used in the examples below, require leading for readability due to their very large x-height. The large x-height diminishes the space between lines making the text more tightly leaded and more difficult to read. The same is true of very widely leaded sans serif faces—the space becomes so generous that the eye needs to focus on the text more carefully.

Identification of a virus thought to cause Acquired Immunodeficiency Syndrome (AIDS) was announced by federal researchers on April 23, 1984. The disease destroys the body's natural immune system and is considered to be ultimately fatal. By the date of discovery, AIDS was estimated to have killed 4,000 Americans.

8/9.6 Auto Leading

Identification of a virus thought to cause Acquired Immunodeficiency Syndrome (AIDS) was announced by federal researchers on April 23, 1984. The disease destroys the body's natural immune system and is considered to be ultimately fatal. By the date of discovery, AIDS was estimated to have killed 4,000 Americans.

8/7.5 Negative Leading
Negative leading yields a very dense texture and readability is diminished.

Identification of a virus thought to cause Acquired Immunodeficiency Syndrome (AIDS) was announced by federal researchers on April 23, 1984. The disease destroys the body's natural immune system and is considered to be ultimately fatal. By the date of discovery, AIDS was estimated to have killed 4,000 Americans.

8/12 Wide Leading

Identification of a virus thought to cause Acquired Immunodeficiency Syndrome (AIDS) was announced by federal researchers on April 23, 1984. The disease destroys the body's natural immune system and is considered to be ultimately fatal. By the date of discovery, AIDS was estimated to have killed 4,000 Americans.

8/15 Extra Wide Leading
Wide leading yields a very airy texture.

The designer can choose the standard paragraph alignments such as flush left, flush right, centered, or justified that are a part of every text processing software. The designer can also combine alignments or choose a variation within an alignment.

Flush left, rag right alignment is often thought to be the most readable form of alignment. This alignment provides the reader with proportional spacing throughout the text lines and avoids the changes of spacing that can occur in justified text. The reader also has a vertical left edge to return to on the next line of type, which enhances the rhythm of reading.

Justified text makes for a firm rectangular texture of type that is texturally pleasing to the eye. The computer attempts to justify each line and when a word cannot be broken by hyphenation the result is uneven word spacing (below right).

Identification of a virus thought to cause Acquired Immunodeficiency Syndrome (AIDS) was announced by federal researchers on April 23, 1984. The disease destroys the body's natural immune system and is considered to be ultimately fatal. By the date of discovery, AIDS was estimated to have killed 4,000 Americans.

Flush Left Alignment

Identification of a virus thought to cause Acquired Immunodeficiency Syndrome (AIDS) was announced by federal researchers on April 23, 1984. The disease destroys the body's natural immune system and is considered to be ultimately fatal. By the date of discovery, AIDS was estimated to have killed 4,000 Americans.

Flush Right Alignment

Identification of a virus thought to cause Acquired Immunodeficiency Syndrome (AIDS) was announced by federal researchers on April 23, 1984. The disease destroys the body's natural immune system and is considered to be ultimately fatal. By the date of discovery, AIDS was estimated to have killed 4,000 Americans.

Centered Alignment

Identification of a virus thought to cause Acquired Immunodeficiency Syndrome (AIDS) was announced by federal researchers on April 23, 1984. The disease destroys the body's natural immune system and is considered to be ultimately fatal. By the date of discovery, AIDS was estimated to have killed 4,000 Americans.

Justified Alignment
The light red rectangles are the width of normal word spacing and show the uneven and excessive word spacing caused by justification.

Constraints:
- One Type Face
- One Size
- One Weight
- Flush Left or Flush Right or Justified

Variables:
- Position
- Leading
- Word Space
- Letter Space
- Alignment

Identification
of the
AIDS Virus

April 23

1984

Identification of a virus thought to
cause Acquired Immunodeficiency
Syndrome (AIDS) was announced by
federal researchers on April 23, 1984.
The disease destroys the body's natural
immune system and is considered to be
ultimately fatal. By the date of discovery, AIDS was estimated to have killed
4,000 Americans.

Variation 1, Hierarchy
1st Order: Title
2nd Order: Day
3rd Order: Year
4th Order: Text

Identification of the AIDS Virus

April 23

1984

Identification of a virus thought to
cause Acquired Immunodeficiency
Syndrome (AIDS) was announced by
federal researchers on April 23, 1984.
The disease destroys the body's natural
immune system and is considered to be
ultimately fatal. By the date of discovery, AIDS was estimated to have killed
4,000 Americans.

Variation 2, Hierarchy
1st Order: Title
2nd Order: Day
3rd Order: Year
4th Order: Text

Identification
of the AIDS Virus

Identification of a virus thought to cause Acquired Immunodeficiency Syndrome (AIDS) was
announced by federal researchers on April 23,
1984. The disease destroys the body's natural
immune system and is considered to be ultimately fatal. By the date of discovery, AIDS was
estimated to have killed 4,000 Americans.

April 23, 1984

Variation 3, Hierarchy
1st Order: Title
2nd Order: Text
3rd Order: Day
4th Order: Year

Identification

of the

AIDS

Virus

April 23

1984

Identification of a vi-
rus thought to cause
Acquired Immuno-
deficiency Syndrome
(AIDS) was announced
by federal researchers
on April 23, 1984. The
disease destroys the
body's natural immune
system and is consid-
ered to be ultimately
fatal. By the date of
discovery, AIDS was
estimated to have killed
4,000 Americans.

Variation 4, Hierarchy
1st Order: Title
2nd Order: Day
3rd Order: Year
4th Order: Text

1 9 8 4

Identification
of the   April 23
AIDS Virus

Identification of a virus thought
to cause Acquired Immunodeficiency Syndrome (AIDS) was announced by federal researchers
on April 23, 1984. The disease
destroys the body's natural immune system and is considered
to be ultimately fatal. By the
date of discovery, AIDS was
estimated to have killed 4,000
Americans.

Variation 5, Hierarchy
1st Order: Year
2nd Order: Title
3rd Order: Day
4th Order: Text

Identification of a virus thought
to cause Acquired Immunodeficiency Syndrome (AIDS) was
announced by federal research-   April 23
ers on April 23, 1984. The dis-   1984
ease destroys the body's

Identification of the AIDS Virus

natural immune system and
is considered to be ultimately
fatal. By the date of discovery,
AIDS was estimated to have
killed 4,000 Americans.

Variation 6, Hierarchy
1st Order: Day
2nd Order: Year
3rd Order: Text
4th Order: Title

---

1   9   8   4

Identification of a virus
thought to cause Acquired
Immunodeficiency Syndrome
(AIDS) was announced by
federal researchers on April
23, 1984. The disease destroys
the body's natural immune
system and is considered to be
ultimately fatal. By the date of
discovery, AIDS was estimated
to have killed 4,000 Americans.

Identification
of the AIDS Virus

April 23

Variation 7, Hierarchy
1st Order: Year
2nd Order: Text
3rd Order: Title
4th Order: Day

Identification of a virus thought
to cause Acquired Immuno-
deficiency Syndrome (AIDS)
was announced by federal researchers on April 23, 1984. The
disease destroys the body's
natural immune system and
is considered to be ultimately
fatal. By the date of discovery,
AIDS was estimated to have
killed 4,000 Americans.

April 23, 1984

Identification of the AIDS Virus

Variation 8, Hierarchy
1st Order: Text
2nd Order: Day
3rd Order: Year
4th Order: Title

Just as type elements must make sense in terms of hierarchy— position, font, spacing, and column width—so, too, must nonobjective elements. Nonobjective elements are usually geometric shapes without meaning, such as the rectangular lines, called rules, shown in the examples below. There are three reasons to use nonobjective elements: 1. emphasis, 2. organization, or 3. balance. When nonobjective elements are used functionally, they enhance and support the meaning of the typographic message. When nonobjective elements do not have a function, they become decorative elements and attract attention away from the meaning of the typographic message.

When rules are used as nonobjective elements, consideration is given to the compositional structure. In the examples, the rule length is determined by the line length. Variation in rule width is used to emphasize hierarchy, and the change from thick to thin creates rhythm and enhances eye flow through the page.

Contemporary American Photographers

The Museum of Modern Art

June 12–15, 2001

Contemporary American Photographers

The Museum of Modern Art

June 12–15, 2001

Contemporary American Photographers

The Museum of Modern Art

June 12–15, 2001

Contemporary American Photographers

The Museum of Modern Art

June 12–15, 2001

Contemporary American Photographers

The Museum of Modern Art

June 12–15, 2001

Contemporary American Photographers

The Museum of Modern Art

June 12–15, 2001

The circle is the most visually powerful geometric shape and the eye is inexorably attracted to it. Even very small circles command considerable attention and must be used sparingly and with care so as not to overpower the composition. Similar to rules, the changes in circle size and repetition create rhythm and directs eye flow. Larger circles can divert attention to a part of a word or to the entire word.

After the hierarchy exercises, an acute awareness of the order of importance of each element in the composition develops. The next phase of learning looks at the development of contrast within the composition. At this point there are many more options than constraints. The complexity of composition increases but so, too, does the dynamic vitality of the work.

The final phase of the project involves the combination of words and images. Found images are used to enhance and emphasize meaning with the focus, again, on maintaining a hierarchy within the composition.

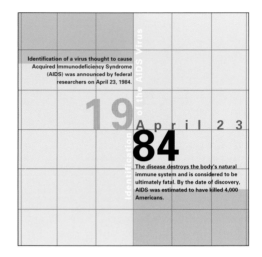

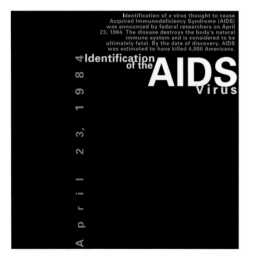

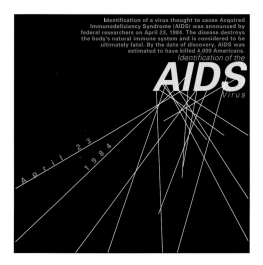

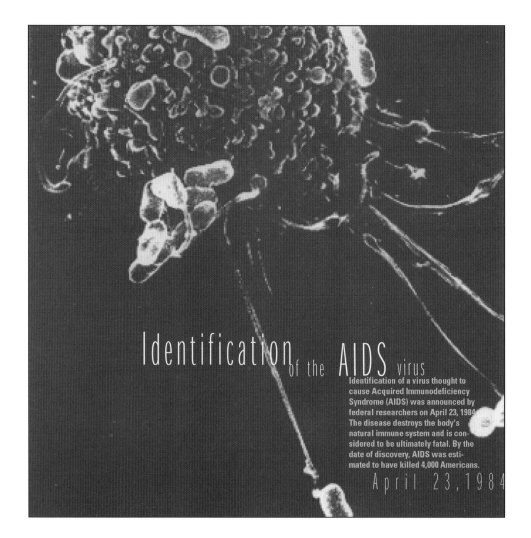

Identification of the AIDS virus

Identification of a virus thought to cause Acquired Immunodeficiency Syndrome (AIDS) was announced by federal researchers on April 23, 1984. The disease destroys the body's natural immune system and is considered to be ultimately fatal. By the date of discovery, AIDS was estimated to have killed 4,000 Americans.

April 23, 1984

Visual Message Content

Title   The Beginning of Communism in Cuba

Day   January 1

Year   1959

Text   Fidel Castro started the Cuban Revolution on January 1, 1959. On this day, he reached the Sierra Maestra Mountains in the eastern part of Cuba. From these mountains he began to lead the harassment of the Batista regime. This was the beginning of Castro's underground movement to overthrow the government.

      Pedro Perez, 1996

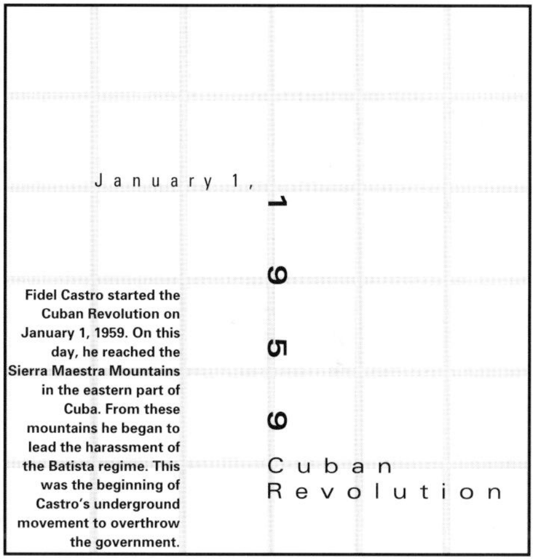

J a n u a r y 1,

1
9
5
9

C u b a n
R e v o l u t i o n

Fidel Castro started the
Cuban Revolution on
January 1, 1959. On this
day, he reached the
Sierra Maestra Mountains
in the eastern part of
Cuba. From these
mountains he began to
lead the harassment of
the Batista regime. This
was the beginning of
Castro's underground
movement to overthrow
the government.

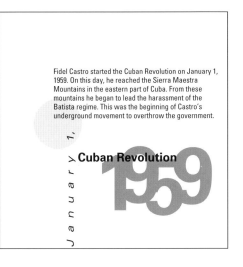

Fidel Castro started the Cuban Revolution on January 1, 1959. On this day, he reached the Sierra Maestra Mountains in the eastern part of Cuba. From these mountains he began to lead the harassment of the Batista regime. This was the beginning of Castro's underground movement to overthrow the government.

Cuban Revolution

January 1, nineteen59

Cuban Revolution

Fidel Castro started the Cuban Revolution on January 1, 1959. On this day, he reached the Sierra Maestra Mountains in the eastern part of Cuba. From these mountains he began to lead the harassment of the Batista regime. This was the beginning of Castro's underground movement to overthrow the government.

1959

January 1,

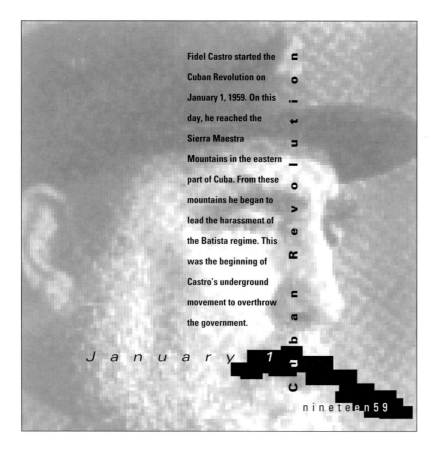

Fidel Castro started the Cuban Revolution on January 1, 1959. On this day, he reached the Sierra Maestra Mountains in the eastern part of Cuba. From these mountains he began to lead the harassment of the Batista regime. This was the beginning of Castro's underground movement to overthrow the government.

Cuban Revolution

January 1

nineteen59

january
1,
1959
the beginning of communism in cuba

Fidel Castro started the Cuban Revolution on January 1, 1959. On this day, he reached the Sierra Maestra Mountains in the eastern part of Cuba. From these mountains he began to lead the harassment of the Batista regime. This was the beginning of Castro's underground movement to overthrow the government.

Visual Message Content

Title   Levi's Become Fashion

Day   September 16

Year   1946

Text   After Levi Strauss introduced rough canvas pants for miners during the gold rush, jeans became the trousers for tough work. During World War I, the demand increased, since people were looking for a sturdy, comfortable garment. In 1946 Levi's introduced jeans in the retail market that were characterized by a red label on the rear right-side pocket.

Christina Archila, 1997

Levi's Become Fashion
1 9 4 6

After Levi Strauss introduced rough canvas pants for miners during the gold rush, jeans became the trousers for tough work. During World War I, the demand increased, since people were looking for a sturdy, comfortable garment. In 1946 the Levi Strauss Co. introduced jeans in the retail market that were characterized by a red label on the rear right-side pocket.

September 16

1 9 4 6

September 16

Levi's Become Fashion

After Levi Strauss introduced rough canvas pants for miners during the gold rush, jeans became the trousers for tough work. During World War I, the demand increased, since people were looking for a sturdy, comfortable garment. In 1946 Levi's introduced jeans in the retail market that were characterized by a red label on the rear right-side pocket.

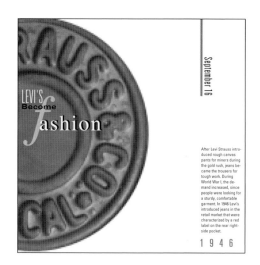

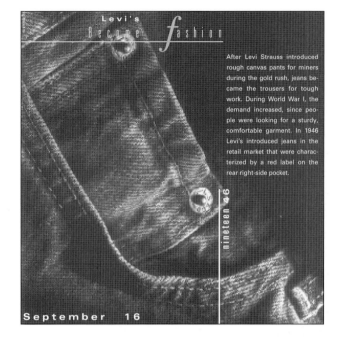

After Levi Strauss introduced rough canvas pants for miners during the gold rush, jeans became the trousers for tough work. During World War I, the demand increased, since people were looking for a sturdy, comfortable garment. In 1946 Levi's introduced jeans in the retail market that were characterized by a red label on the rear right-side pocket.

After Levi Strauss introduced rough canvas pants for miners during the gold rush, jeans became the trousers for tough work. During World War I, the demand increased, since people were looking for a sturdy, comfortable garment. In 1946 Levi's introduced jeans in the retail market that were characterized by a red label on the rear right-side pocket.

Visual Message Content

Title   "If the glove don't fit, you must acquit."

Day   October 3

Year   1995

Text   The media circus labeled it "the trial of the century," and it mesmerized the nation. On October 3, 1995, O. J. Simpson was acquitted in the slayings of his ex-wife, Nicole Brown, and Ronald Goldman. As a result of all of the surrounding hype, there were book deals, a glove, "court TV," catch phrases, a racist Mark Fuhrman, and, often forgotten, two victims. The acquittal ended a 372-day trial of murder, domestic violence, and allegations of police misconduct.

John Pietrafesa, 1998

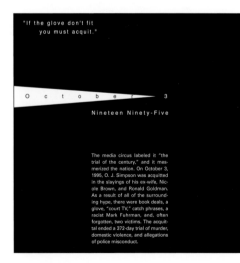

October 3
nineteen ninety-five

"If the glove don't **fit** you must **acquit**"

Reasonable Doubt

The media circus labeled it "the trial of the century," and it mesmerized the nation. On October 3, 1995, O. J. Simpson was acquitted in the slayings of his ex-wife, Nicole Brown, and Ronald Goldman. As a result of all of the surrounding hype, there were book deals, a glove, "court TV," catch phrases, a racist Mark Fuhrman, and, often forgotten, two victims. The acquittal ended a 372-day trial of murder, domestic violence, and allegations of police misconduct.

Acknowledgments

Special thanks to Benjamin Watters and Syreeta Pitts for research, layout, and administrative assistance and to the Ringling School of Art and Design, Faculty and Staff Development Grant Committee.

Students from the Ringling School of Art and Design who have contributed work include:

Mina Ajrab
Christina Archila
Kathy Azada
Jana Dee Bassingthwaite
Drew Chibbaro
Arthur Gilo
Amy Goforth
Erin Kaman
Lora Kanetzky
James De Mass, Jr.

Hans Mathre
Ashley McCulloch
Will Miller
Rusty Morris
Pedro Perez
Sara Petti
John Pietrafesa
Drew Tyndell
Wood D. Weber

FEB 4 2009

Image Credits

Best Swiss Posters of the Year 1992, Siegfried Odermatt

Columbia University, Graduate School of Architecture and Planning Posters, Willi Kunz, New York

Columbia University, Graduate School of Architecture and Planning, Lecture and Exhibition Posters, Willi Kunz, New York

Festival d'été (Summer Festival), Program Spread, Philippe Apeloig

Institute for Architecture and Urban Studies Graphic Program, Massimo Vignelli

National-Zeitung (Newspaper) Poster Series, Karl Gerstner

Nike ACG Pro Purchase Catalog, Angelo Colleti, Shellie Anderson

Program for Zurich University's 150th Anniversary, Siegfried Odermatt

SamataMason Web Site, Kevin Kruger

Sotheby's Graphic Program, Massimo Vignelli

Selected Bibliography

Celant, Germano. *Design: Vignelli*. New York: Rizzoli International Publications, Inc., 1990.

Codrington, Andrea, ed. *AIGA: 365, AIGA Year in Design 22*. New York: Distributed Art Publishers, Inc., 2002.

50 Years: Swiss Posters Selected by the Federal Department of Home Affairs, 1941–1990. Geneva: Societe Generale d'Affichage in collaboration with Kummerly & Frey AG Berne, 1991.

Gottschall, Edward M. *Typographic Communications Today*. Cambridge, MA: The MIT Press, 1989.

Kröplien, Manfred, ed. *Karl Gerstner, Review of 5 x 10 Years of Graphic Design Etc*. Ostfildern-Ruit: Hatje Cantz Verlag, 2001.

Kunz, Willi. *Typography: Formation + TransFormation*. Sulgen, Switzerland: Verlag Niggli AG and Willi Kunz Books, 2003.

Kunz, Willi. *Typography: Macro- + Micro-Aesthetics, Fundamentals of Typographic Design*. Sulgen, Switzerland: Verlag Niggli AG and Willi Kunz Books, 2000.

Müller-Brockmann, Josef. *The Graphic Artist and His Design Problems*. Teufen, Switzerland: Arthur Niggi Ltd., 1961.

Müller-Brockmann, Josef. *A History of Visual Communication*. New York: Hastings House, 1971.

Ruder, Emil. *Typographie, Typography*. Heiden, Switzerland: Arthur Niggli Ltd., 1977.

Spencer, Herbert. *Pioneers of Modern Typography*. Revised edition. Cambridge, MA: The MIT Press, 1983.

Tschichold, Jan. *Asymmetric Typography*. Toronto: Cooper & Beatty, 1967.

Waser, Jack and Werner M. Wolf. *Odematt & Tissi, Graphic Design*. Zurich: J. E. Wolfensberger AG, 1993.

A
alignment, 99
Apeloig, Philippe
    Festival d'été, 68
Archila, Christina, 112–15
axial alignment, 18–21, 24–26, 29–31, 47,
    50–51, 53–54, 56–57, 59–60, 73, 79,
    82, 85
axial relationships, 12
Azada, Kathy, 97, 104-6

B
balance, circle, 14–15
Bauhaus products, catalog of, 37
Bayer, Herbert
    Bauhaus products, catalog of, 37
    Kandinsky poster, 89
Beginning of Communism in Cuba, 107–11
Berlewi, Henryk
    The Next Call, 90
    Reklama Mechano, 90
The Best Swiss Posters of the Year 1992, 67

C
case study
    Beginning of Communism in Cuba,
        107–11
    Identification of the AIDS Virus, 97,
        104–6
    "If the glove don't fit, you must
        acquit," 116–17
    Levi's Become Fashion, 112–15
circle and composition, 14–15
circle placement, 18–21, 24–26, 29–31
Colletti, Angelo
    Nike ACG Pro Purchase catalog, 64–65
Columbia University, Graduate School of
    Architecture and Planning, 69, 94–95
Columbia University, Graduate School of
    Architecture and Planning, lecture
    and exhibition posters, 94–95
Columbia University, Graduate School of
    Architecture and Planning posters, 69
constraints and options, 8

D
diagonal composition, 71–87
    direction and contrast, 72
    grid placement, 74–75
    organizing the approach to the project, 73
    thumbnails
        contrasting directions 30°/60°, 85
        contrasting directions 45°/45°, 79
        single direction 30° or 60°, 82
        single direction 45°, 76
    type replacement
        contrasting directions 30°/60°,
            86–87
        contrasting directions 45°/45°, 80–81

single direction 30° or 60°, 83–84
single direction 45°, 77–78
Die Neue Typographie, 35
Drenttel Doyle Partners
    The New Urban Landscape, 45

E
edge tension, 73, 79, 85

F
Festival d'été, 68
Freiburg Municipal Theatre, 92–93

G
Gassner, Christof
    Theatre Am Hechtplatz, 38–39
Gerstner, Karl
    National-Zeitung, 91
grouping, 10–11, 18–21, 29–31, 47, 50–51,
    53–54, 56–57, 59–60, 73, 79, 82, 85

H
hierarchy
    proportion, 9
hierarchy, typographic, 97–117
    alignment, 99
    compositions, 100–1
    leading, 98
    rules and nonobjective elements,
        102–3
horizontal composition, 17–33
    critique
        long rectangle in bottom position, 26
        long rectangle in interior position, 31
        long rectangle in top position, 21
    organizing the approach to the project, 18
    thumbnails
        long rectangle in bottom position,
            24–25
        long rectangle in interior position,
            29–30
        long rectangle in top position, 19–20
    type replacement
        long rectangle in bottom position,
            27–28
        long rectangle in interior position,
            32–33
        long rectangle in top position, 22–23
horizontal/vertical composition, 46–61
    organizing the approach to the
        project, 47
    reading direction, 49
    rotation of composition, 48
    thumbnails
        long rectangle in bottom position,
            53–54
        long rectangle in interior position,
            59–60
        long rectangle in left or right

position, 56–57
    long rectangle in top position, 50–51
type replacement
    long rectangle in interior position, 61
    long rectangle in left or right
        position, 58
    long rectangle in top or bottom
        position, 56
    long rectangle in top position, 52

I
Identification of the AIDS Virus, 97–101,
    104–6
"If the glove don't fit, you must acquit,"
    116–17
Institute for Architecture and Urban Studies
    Graphic Program, 42–43
The Isms of Art, 36

K
Kandinsky poster, 89
Krueger, Kevin
    SamataMason, 40
Kunz, Willi
    Columbia University, Graduate School of
        Architecture and Planning, 69, 94–95

L
law of thirds, 5, 13, 18–21, 24–26, 29–31,
    47, 50–51, 53–54, 56–57, 59–60, 73, 79,
    82, 85
leading, 18–21, 24–26, 29–31, 47, 50–51,
    53–54, 56–57, 59–60, 73, 79, 82, 85,
    98, 100
Levi's Become Fashion, 112–15
Lissitzky, El
    The Isms of Art, 36
Lohse, Richard P.
    Zürcher Künstler im Helmhaus poster, 63

M
Mason, Dave
    SamataMason, 40–41

N
National-Zeitung, 91
negative space, 11, 18–21, 24–26, 29–31, 47,
    50–51, 53–54, 56–57, 59–60, 73, 79,
    82, 85
    negative space and grouping, 11
The New Urban Landscape, 45
The Next Call, 90
Nike ACG Pro Purchase catalog, 64–65
nonobjective elements, 102–3

O
Odermatt & Tissi
    The Best Swiss Posters of the Year 1992,
        67

program for Zurich University 150th
    anniversary, 66
organization, circle, 14–15

P
Perez, Pedro, 107–11
perimeter edge, 12, 18–21, 24–26, 29–31, 47,
    50–51, 53–54, 56–57, 59–60, 73, 79,
    82, 85
    axial relationships, 12
Pietrafesa, John, 116–17
pivot point, circle, 14–15
project elements and process, 7
proportion of elements, 9

R
reading direction, 47, 49, 76, 92
Reklama Mechano, 90
rotation of composition, 48
Ruder, Emil
    Freiburg Municipal Theatre, 92–93
rules and nonobjective elements, 102–3

S
SamataMason Web Site, 40–41
Sotheby's Graphic Program, 44
space activator, circle, 14–15
starting or stopping point, circle, 14–15

T
tension, circle, 14–15
Theatre Am Hechtplatz, 38–39
Tschichold, Jan
    Die Neue Typographie, 35
typographic hierarchy, 97–117

V
Verdine, Michael
    Nike ACG Pro Purchase catalog, 64–65
Vignelli and Associates
    Institute for Architecture and Urban
        Studies Graphic Program, 42–43
    Sotheby's Graphic Program, 44

W
Werkman, H. N.
    The Next Call, 90
wild-card element, circle, 7

Z
Zürcher Künstler im Helmhaus poster, 63
Zurich University 150th anniversary, 66